# SCAR SONGS

## W. ROYCE ADAMS

ISBN:   979-8-9909378-6-4 (Paperback)
        979-8-9913091-7-2 (E-book)

Library of Congress Control Number: 2023900081

Published By:

Santa Barbara, CA 93103
www.rjkbooks.com

Publisher Provider:

Children show scars like medals.
Lovers use them as secrets to reveal. A scar is what
happens when the word is made flesh.

—Leonard Cohen


Contrary to what we may have been taught,
unnecessary and unchosen suffering wounds us but
need not scar us for life. It does mark. What we allow
the mark to become is in our own hands.

—Bell Hooks


Some scars don't hurt. Some scars are numb. Some
scars rid you of the capacity to feel anything ever again.

—Joyce Rachelle

# CONTENTS

Life's lessons are bitter ways to sweetness.

—Herman J. Steinherr

# THIEF CATCHER

At the age of sixteen, I worked after school and on Saturdays at Kroger's Grocery. I stuffed customers' purchases into brown bags, unloaded supply trucks, stacked heavy boxes on a hand dolly and wheeled them around like a graceful dancer, stamped prices robot-like on canned goods, and stocked them on the shelves as fast as customers removed them. I learned to trim and spray water on produce to make items like lettuce look fresh on display. A no-brainer job really, but it came with a uniform—a long, white, around-the-neck apron—and a box cutter.

While I enjoyed the work and the routines, there was a part to that job that after all these years still causes me some unease.

The store had a high ceiling, and only the staff knew of the passageway hidden behind the advertisements and sales posters covering three walls. Periodically and strategically placed along the passageway were peepholes that allowed views of different sections of the store, making it possible to watch any customer's movements. It was referred to as "The Watch Tower."

One day, Dave, the manager of the store in his white butcher cap and around-the-neck apron, stopped me from stamping prices on cans of Del Monte corn and gave me another task.

"See that woman with the long, dark dress over near the cereal aisle?" he asked.

She was hard to miss. It was summer, yet she wore a dark brown dress with long sleeves and a skirt that nearly reached the floor. Her hair was lost in some kind of a colorful turban wrapped around her head. She shuffled about, a bit bent over, and seemed to me just an old lady who had trouble walking.

I assured Dave I saw her.

"Get up in the Tower and keep an eye on her. She's acting strange."

This was a new part of the job. I'd never been up in the Tower before. The idea of spying on someone offered more excitement than stamping prices on cans. I felt as if some secret privilege and power had been granted me. So up I went, my heartbeat accelerating in anticipation.

I found the best spots in the hidden passageway to keep an eye on the woman in the dark dress as she moved about. Down below me, the entire store spread out like a huge colored map. Like most chain grocery stores, Kroger's had wide glass windows at the front entrance covered with huge posters promoting weekly specialties; several checkout counters as you entered; seven or eight long aisles of tempting, multicolored packaged goods from the floor up; a meat market counter case running along the left wall all the way to back doors hiding the freezer; a produce section stacked with fruit and vegetables taking up the wall on the right; and swinging doors in the back of the store where goods were stored, along with a walk-in refrigerated section to store and protect the produce from getting brown too fast. I worked down there where people were milling about, and I felt a sense of pride. I was protecting my domain. And no one could see me.

That's when it occurred to me. Had Dave or some employee ever spied on me while I worked?

As I watched my prey, I noticed that sometimes the woman would look around to see if anyone was near. If the aisle was devoid of customers, she seemed to have no trouble walking, but as soon as she was within sight of others, her walking reverted to an appearance of struggle. I wondered if Dave had noticed this and if that was why he sent me up there.

I observed her for several minutes. She took her time going up and down the aisles, stopping and examining an item here and there, then putting it back on the shelf. She would open the glass door of the frozen food section, stare inside, then close the fogged-up door without taking anything out. I began to think that maybe she had just come to the store to get out of the heat and enjoy the air conditioning.

But then in the soap and notions aisle, her actions became clear.

For about the fourth time, she stopped in front of the various boxes of soap on display.

She looked around, saw no one, grabbed a medium-size box of Rinso, lifted her skirt, placed the box between her thighs, and dropped her skirt. It happened so fast, it took a moment to convince myself of what I saw, and I let out a little laugh.

She looked around to make certain no one had seen her and resumed her troubled walk.

Rather than leave the store, as I thought she now might, she went down the next aisle and grabbed a can of Campbell soup. Where was she going to hide that? But she surprised me and hobbled her way to the shortest checkout line.

I snapped to the realization that I was witnessing a possible shoplifting, and my job now was to run down from the Tower and tell Dave what I had seen. Since it looked as if she was going to pay for the can of soup, I had time, but, excited at what I had discovered, I went down the steps two at a time. When I reached the bottom, I searched down each aisle, trying to find Dave. Then I saw him standing near the butcher counter, his eyes already on the woman ready to steal a box of soap powder.

I tried waving my arms to get his attention, but he didn't see me, so I tried to look casual as I approached him. As I got closer, he noticed me, gave me a furtive look, but his eyes went back to watching the woman.

"Well?" he asked, not looking at me.

"Yeah. She took a box of Rinso."

Then his look questioned me. "Rinso? Where's she hiding a box of Rinso?"

"Between her legs. Under her skirt," I said in an amused, can-you-believe-it tone.

His eyebrows furrowed as he nodded. "Aha. Good work. OK. Go back to what you were doing. I'll take care of this."

Well, I didn't want to go back to what I was doing. I had caught a thief in the act, and I wanted to be in on the confrontation about to occur. But I didn't want to get fired, either. So I went back to the canned corn-tomatoes-peas-beans-hominy aisle with frequent looks back at Dave as he stood near the door our soap thief lady would have to exit. Unaccountably, the advertising jingle "Rinso white, Rinso bright, Happy little washday song!" started jamming in my head.

The opened box of canned corn I had been price stamping was way down the aisle, so I couldn't see what was happening at the checkout counter. To continue my spying, I moved the box of canned goods I was stamping toward the opening of the aisle where I could see what was about to transpire.

I watched as our Rinso thief paid for the Campbell soup and shuffled her way toward the exit. Before she got to the door, Dave stopped her.

"I believe you have forgotten to pay for the Rinso."

"What?" the woman said, looking around, startled.

"Come on, now," Dave said. "We saw you take it."

"I… I…" the woman started to say something but never finished and started crying and moaning.

Now, from where I was positioned, I couldn't see everything that happened, but here's what I put together.

She dropped her small bag with the can of soup. The box of Rinso made a slight plop as it fell from between her thighs to the floor. Dave looked down and then jumped back, muttering something like "Oh Christ" as the woman yanked up her dress about twelve inches and tried to spread her feet as a puddle of pee began to form on the floor and on the dented box of Rinso.

I left my post and dashed to the front of the store. What I saw is a tableau forever burned in my memory: Gloria, the red-haired cashier, who had just unknowingly checked out the soap thief, stands with her back to the cash register, both hands covering her opened mouth, her eyes glued to the floor. The two customers in the checkout lane are peering around each other, trying to see what is happening. Dave stands there in his white butcher cap and apron, his managerial skills abandoned for the moment, staring at the box of Rinso getting peed on. The soap thief's face shows a combination of embarrassment, fear, and a look that says she would rather be anywhere in the world but where she was, doing what she was.

"Rinso white! Rinso bright!"

Tableau over, Dave took off his butcher cap, revealing to me for the first time that he was bald. He scratched his head, flapped the cap against his thigh, and muttered, "God Almighty, lady! What the hell?"

Gloria, not understanding yet that the woman was stealing, felt sorry for the thief and offered her a box of Kleenex from under the counter. The woman was too traumatized to move. One of the women customers waiting to check out left her items on the counter and rushed out the door. Dave, putting his cap back on and regaining his managerial skills, yelled to anyone listening, "Get a mop and bucket! Clean this mess up. And Gloria, call the police!"

For some reason, I believed he wanted me to get the mop and bucket. I hated to leave the scene of the crime, but being a dutiful employee, I rushed to the back storeroom and spent too much time finding them. By the time I returned to the front of the store, Dave, the Rinso lady, and two policemen were outside the store, writing up my spy work.

The bucket, of course, was empty and of no help. I remembered a faucet and hose outside that we used to clean off the sidewalk after unloading trucks, so I took the bucket outside and started filling it. The group fell silent when they saw me, and I realized they weren't going to continue until I left. Why weren't they asking me questions? I was the one who caught her. The woman, upon a closer look, appeared to be about my mother's age. She looked at me with hurt eyes, and I wondered if they told her I was the one who saw her steal the soap.

Back inside the store after filling the bucket, I looked out the window and watched the police take her away.

At first mop, I didn't feel it was my job to clean up her mess. Then I thought, well, maybe it was. I did spy on her. I did tell Dave about her. I'm the one who caused her to be arrested. But who was she? Why did she pay for a can of soup but try to steal a box of soap powder? Was she so poor she needed to steal soap? Did she have kids to feed? Had she stolen before? Did she have a history of theft? Would they really put her in jail for stealing a box of soap? Yes, I'd caught a thief, but I didn't feel at all good about it. In fact, I now felt sorry for her and wished I'd never been sent to the Tower.

I went back to stamping prices on cans of corn, and halfway through, I realized I was stamping the wrong price.

Just then, Dave approached me.

"Good job. Well done."

He put his hand on my shoulder. I didn't know whether he meant my mopping or being a spy.

"What's going to happen to her?" I asked.

"Don't know," he said. "Depends on her record. Anyway, not our problem now."

*Oh?* I thought, looking down at the cans of corn. *Maybe not yours.*

Grief is just love with no place to go.

—Jamie Anderson

# THE LAST TEQUILA RUN

Our technique was simple. We would cross the border at Tijuana, visiting several liquor stores so as not to create suspicion, buying up dozens of bottles of Jose Cuervo tequila. In those days, it was illegal to take more than three liters of alcohol across the border. I don't know who we thought might be suspicious, but worrying that someone could be watching made the venture more thrilling. Then we would find a remote spot and, bottle by bottle, start filling Robert's phony ten-gallon gas tank he'd installed under his Ford F-1 pickup truck. We saved a few empty bottles to refill and sell or pass around at dorm parties back home.

Once loaded with our hidden contraband, we would head down to Punta Banda, back in the early '50s just a rocky, barren, isolated place to camp and fish. Our routine was to start drinking once we left Tijuana, making sure the level of the liquid had fallen to the crow's feet on the label. This usually got us as far as Ensenada, where the Mexican border patrol had a small station requiring travelers to stop and sign in for permission to continue farther south.

Perhaps because we had done these runs before, or more likely because we had dropped the level of the tequila in the bottle below the crow's feet, Robert decided not to stop this time at the border station and drive on through to our usual camping spot.

"We need to set up camp... you know... before dark." He hunched his tall, muscular body over the steering wheel and looked at me to see my reaction. His speech and blue eyes showed the effects of the tequila. Shit, did I look as wasted?

"Not a good idea, man. We'd better stop. It only takes a couple minutes." I was drunk, but not that drunk.

"Naw, it'll be," Robert assured me. He had on a tight, white T-shirt that emphasized his tanned arms. He kept leaning forward, like he was going to leap at something, the muscles in his arms tightening on and off as he kept squeezing the wheel.

"I dunno, man."

"Don't be a pussy."

One of his favorite words: *pussy*. He used it to refer to many things, but most often at me when I didn't like one of his schemes. Physically, he was bigger than me, bolder, and almost a year older than my twenty. Sometimes I questioned why he liked me. We'd met as freshman at UCLA two years before and hit it off, rented an apartment together, took the same classes, did homework together when we did homework, crashed the same parties, usually told each other everything. But he was "the man," you know, the big Kahuna. Everybody liked him, because he said what he wanted in a non-threatening way and showed no sense of fear. Robert Redford handsome, funny, smart, a charmer. A magnet for women. And I often benefited from that by merely being with him. I felt flattered he let me hang out with him because I had none of his attributes. I thought of myself as a kind of remora runner, involved in the swim of things, attaching myself to his glow, but never the big fish. Sometimes I felt like his mascot. Not that he treated me that way. Never. It's just the way I saw myself sometimes when I compared myself to him. I enjoyed my status, a bit like a little brother who looks up to his big brother. Alcohol, however, was his Achilles heel.

As we drove past the border station, Robert showed his white teeth and waved congenially to the authorities waiting for us to stop.

"See. Told ya, no problem." Robert grinned, peering in the rearview mirror.

It didn't take long for our tequila-bloated brains to become conscious of an official car of some kind trailing us, lights flashing and siren screaming. We realized, even in our loss of good sense, it meant pull over.

I worried Robert wouldn't stop. Thankfully, he did.

"Be cool. I'll explain," he said.

Before either of us could say anything, we each had an armed Mexican *federale* at our window, pointing guns at us.

*"Fuera del carro! Fuera del carro!"* the men yelled.

"Uh-oh. Guess they want to see our stinkin' badges," Robert said, laughing.

A fuzzy sobriety came over me. "Not funny, man! I think they want us to get out of the truck. Don't be a smart ass. They'll fuckin' shoot us."

At that moment, knowing Robert, I was more worried he'd pull some nutty stunt and get us both killed.

"Shit, now we'll never get there before dark," Robert slurred, still sitting in the truck.

"Come on. Just get out … and keep your hands up." I opened my door and stumbled out.

Robert took his time but managed to step out, his hands halfway up, and give the men a big smile.

"Hola," Robert offered, pronouncing and emphasizing the letter H.

This did not endear us to the officers in charge.

One of them, short and pudgy enough to stretch the buttons on his brown uniform shirt, said something in angry Spanish I didn't understand. When I didn't move, he yelled it again and motioned with his gun for me to go to the driver's side of the truck and stand beside Robert, who was having trouble balancing. When I did as instructed, the other officer, taller and apparently the one in charge, held his gun on us while he ordered his partner to inspect the truck.

"Well, this is the shits," Robert muttered. "Hope they don't find the booze."

"Oh great. Just tell 'em where it is, why doncha?" I whispered.

*"Silencio!"* the tall one yelled. *"Arriba las manos!"* By now, he could see we were gringos.

"Hands up!" He pointed his head upward.

I don't know how long we stood there swaying with our hands up, but it was long enough for it to feel painful and for the searching officer to go through our camping stuff shoved in the camper shell.

He came out of the truck cabin holding three empty bottles and the almost-empty one we would later blame for our predicament.

Something was said to the officer holding a gun on us, but my college Spanish being fragile at best, I only caught *muy* and *borracho*.

I guess it showed.

The two officers spoke to each other, argued about something, and then seemed to agree on what to do with us.

"Speak Spanish?' the leader asked.

"Not me," Robert said, his arms drifting down. "Not a word." He did speak some, of course, but was being a stubborn drunk.

"Up—hands." The leader used his gun to point up and then back at us.

"You." He looked at me. "Speak Spanish?"

I reviewed my two semesters of Spanish as best I could. "Me? *No mucho.*"

Then I tried, "*No comprendo muy* … no … *muchas* … yeah … *muchas palabras.*" I felt pretty sure I hadn't said that right.

He shook his head in disgust. "Why you here? Drugs?" the leader asked, ignoring my language facilities.

"We love your country." Robert emphasized *love*.

"*Qué?*"

"To camp and fish," I injected. I'd used up all the Spanish I could remember.

"And drink tequila," Robert added, trying to make a joke of our situation. "*Mucho* drinko."

He ignored Robert's comment. "*Dondé campamento?*"

I think I understood what he asked.

"Camping? Punta Banda. Many times."

"Many times?"

"Yeah. I mean, *si*. Many, many times." My arms were killing me.

"Why you no stopped at sign? Many times you no stopped, eh?"

"No. No. We always stop. Always."

"Yeah," Robert chimed in. "Yeah, we always stop-ped. Always. We stop-ped, for sure." I wanted to knock Robert in the head for his mimicking. His charm wasn't working here. "You think this funny?" The lawman stepped toward Robert, and I thought he might hit Robert for me.

Robert looked down at the gun near his stomach and at last seemed to wake up to our situation.

"No, no, no, man. This is not funny. Definitely not. Far, far from funny." Then added, "Sorry, man, OK?"

"Why you no stopped?" I was asked again.

"We thought, you know, since we've done this before maybe we didn't really need to stop." Pathetic: the best I could command in my condition.

"Yeah. We're, like, in a hurry to get to our campsite before dark." Robert pointed toward the sky as if that said it all.

I just blurted it out. "We're drunk … *borracho*," then added, to show respect, "sir." The other border guard clinked the empty bottles together, punctuating my confession. The two lawmen conferred for a few minutes, then the leader gave us orders.

"You and you." He waved his gun toward the patrol car. "In back. *Con rapidez!*" We knew then they weren't going to let us go on our way.

"What about my truck?" Robert's face showed he was beginning to understand our situation.

"*Dame las llaves.*" The other officer held out one hand; his other, he placed on the gun in his holster.

Robert looked at me, puzzled. I'd never seen him so nonplussed, and in the unusual moment, I felt more in control than Robert.

"He wants your keys."

Robert hesitated but only for a moment, then yielded. "In the truck." Then he asked the officer, "You gonna drive it? Where ya gonna take it?" He didn't like the idea. I'd never seen Robert losing control.

No answer came, but they finally let us put our hands down only to handcuff us together and put us in the back seat of their car. No one said anything as we were driven back to the patrol station where, earlier, we had spritely waved our way through. Robert kept looking out the back window, making sure his truck was being driven behind us.

Once back at the station, they uncuffed us, demanded our wallets, and placed us in a small room with two chairs and a small table. One small, dirty window sat high on one wall. The green paint peeling off the walls showed many yellow splotches underneath, and a naked light bulb dangled by tangled wiring from the ceiling. While my stomach wanted to heave away all the Cuervo, my bladder demanded first attention while my mind became attentive to the grave situation we had liquefied our way into.

Before they left us alone, I said what was true to the rotund officer. "Sir, I have to pee."

"Yeah, me, too, really bad," Robert said.

"*Qué?*" The man looked blank.

"Pee. Piss. Urinate. You know …" Robert held his hand to his crotch and tried to mimic the action.

Hesitant at first, they took us, again at gunpoint, around to the back of the building, and we gave our business to nature. Then they took us back to the room and shut us in.

We could hear the men in the outer room talking, but my Spanish was no match for theirs. We assumed they were explaining to the others how they had caught two stupid Americano gringo banditos trying to get away from some caper we had pulled.

"Jesus." Robert sat in one of the chairs, rubbing the wrist that had been handcuffed. "What d'ya think they're gonna to do?"

"Don't ask me," I answered. "This is Mexico, man. You've heard stories." "What's the penalty for running through a border stop?"

"How should I know? This is my first smuggling offense." I held my tongue that so wanted to blame him for our predicament.

Then I let it loose. "Why the hell didn't you stop?"

"What if they discover my hidden tank?"

"Arrest us for booze running, probably. That, on top of not stopping at a border."

"But we haven't smuggled anything yet. We bought it all here."

"Still, hiding it in a secret tank? Suspicious maybe?"

"Yeah, they could warn our own border patrol when we go back. That's booze running or something. They could set us up, you know."

"If they let us go."

That sobering "if thought" kept us quiet for a moment, our imaginations going wild in fear.

"Could they keep my truck? You know. For not stopping?" His face showed something I'd never seen in him before: loss of confidence.

"Maybe. How do I know? Think about it. We look suspicious running the border like we did. It looks to them like we were ... I don't know ... trying to get away from something.

Maybe they think we're drug dealers or robbed a store or a bank. Hell, I don't know." We both went silent again.

Then my scared-to-death situation turned back to Robert, and I let loose again. "Why'd you run through like that anyway? Why didn't you stop? You know we're supposed to stop. That was really stupid!"

"Hey, I didn't hear you say stop. You were in just as much a hurry as I was. You could have said 'stop-ped.'"

"Not funny, Robert!" The fact he could make a joke at this point made me even angrier and more sober sick.

"Well, why didn't you say something?"

"I tried, remember?"

"Maybe if I offered them some tequila, they'd let us go."

"Oh sure. Why don't you just do that? Show 'em your—"

That's when the door opened, and the tall patrolman who had held his gun on us and a more official-looking man, with a thick mustache and bars on his shirt epaulets, came in the room.

The official one, looking at one of the driver's license taken from our wallets, asked, "Who Robert Barker?"

"Me." Robert stood up and reached for his license, but it wasn't offered.

"And you..." He read the other license. "How you say, Ray Danner?"

That was good enough for me. "Yes, sir."

He looked at us both, shaking his head. Then he broke out in pretty fair English. "You give no respect for our country. You come here, get drunk, and break laws. You like us come your country, do that?"

He didn't expect an answer, but Robert shook his head in affirmation.

He went on. "We are poor country but demand respect of law. You drunks show no respect. We no want you here. We wait report on you. Maybe you steal truck, yes?"

"No, no. It's mine," Robert blurted out. "The registration's in the glove box. Check it out."

"We soon see." The officer said. He looked angry. Then the two men left the room. "Oh Christ, they're going to keep my truck!"

I didn't say anything because, at this point, I believed the worst. I more worried about me than his damn truck.

The more sober we got, the longer it took for time to pass by. We fell silent, lost in our own personal worries about what could happen to us.

"They could put us in a federal prison, ya know?" I said, half-aloud.

"For what? The tequila?"

"No. For running the border."

"Shit, they could, couldn't they?" Robert got up and walked around. "No. Wait. We crossed the border in TJ legally."

"Yeah, but we ran this checkpoint or whatever you call it. That's just as illegal. That's like a border. They could jail us for that."

I could see the thought hit him. "Nobody would know, would they? We'd never be heard from again."

"Yeah. Or they could put us on a work farm. Make us, like, slaves. I read some countries do that."

"Does anybody know you're here?" he asked.

"No. You?"

"No. Fuck. They could kill us, make our bodies disappear. Or sell our body parts. Keep our stuff, sell my truck. Sell it for parts, too." He paused. "My tequila." He started pacing the room. "Shit! Shit! Shit!"

"You and your damn tequila."

"I gotta get back by Tuesday," he said, like an afterthought.

"What?"

He looked at me kind of sheepishly. "Gotta get back by Tuesday," he repeated, louder.

"Why? What's Tuesday?"

Before Robert could respond, the officer and another border patrolman burst through the door and threw our wallets and the truck keys on the table. "You go now."

Shocked at the abruptness, neither Robert nor I moved.

"We're free to go?" Robert asked, to make sure we heard right. "You go home," the officer said.

"Home?" I said. I felt a not-trustworthy relief. "No camping?"

"No camping. You go home. No come back. Ever."

Robert and I looked at each other, then picked up our wallets. This was too easy.

Something didn't feel right, yet I was ready to split *muy* pronto.

"Look, we're sorry we caused all this confusion. We apologize." Robert pulled a ten- dollar bill from his wallet. "Here. Take this as a peace offering. Our apology."

The officer looked at the bill, then at Robert. "You no buy your way here. Maybe I arrest you for"—he searched for the word—"bribe."

"No!" Robert almost yelled. "No, no, no. No bribe. For being sorry, for apology. Like a... a fine," he said, falling into pidgin English. "We sorry."

Robert stuck the bill out and the officer hesitated, then grabbed it.

"For fine. No bribe." The bill disappeared into his pocket. "Go! Now!" The officer pointed to the door.

"No camping?" Robert asked again.

"No camping. Go now!" he scowled.

We could see there would be no camping and didn't much care at this point. Relieved to be free, we headed back toward the Tijuana-California border. For a short time, we noticed someone in a car following us to make sure of our direction.

"Shit, man, I can't believe they just let us go."

"I knew if I gave him money they'd let us be on our way."

"Bull tacos. He was letting us go anyway. Offering money almost added to our troubles, man."

"Well, it was worth a shot. He took the money. Thought he might let us camp.

Too tired to argue, I just shook my aching head and leaned back against the seat. I closed my eyes. I wanted to sleep but wasn't sure how awake or sober Robert was for the drive back, so I thought I'd better keep him awake.

"What's Tuesday?" I asked, remembering his earlier comment.

"Hmm?"

"Tuesday. You said you have to get back by Tuesday."

"Yeah. I have to report for duty."

"Duty? What duty? You didn't sign on for Duggan's geology field trip, did you? I thought we agreed not to. That's three days stompin' around in Carrizo Plains, man."

"Naw. I was gonna tell you in Punta Banda. I signed up. The marines."

"The marines?"

He nodded.

"The marines. You signed up for the goddamn marines and didn't tell me?" He nodded.

"Why? I mean …"

"My draft number's up. Come on. We talked about it. Always said I'd rather be in the marines than the army."

"Yeah, but just talk. You don't know your number's up for sure. Mine could come up before yours."

"I can feel it, man. My number is comin' up."

"Bullshit."

"Well, I did it. I'm reporting in on Tuesday."

"Thanks for sharing, asshole."

We stayed quiet for a few miles. "Why didn't you tell me?"

He shrugged his shoulders. "I told you. I was going to. After we set up camp. Which we're not now."

"You coulda told me before."

"Ah, did I hurt my pussy buddy's feelings?" He tried that winning smile.

"Fuckin' A, man. You did. You have."

"Look, it was kind of a spur of the moment thing, but I've been thinkin' about it for some time. This Korean crap is hanging over our heads, knowing they're gonna tag us soon. If I have to fight in some friggin' war not of my making, I wanna do it on my terms. I just want to get it over with. No more waiting, you know? In, then out. Over and done."

"But now you're in for four years. What about finishing school?"

"It'll wait. School's not goin' anywhere."

A few more miles of silence.

"If I'd told you, you would've joined up, too. I know it."

"You don't know. Maybe. I don't particularly want to go into the army, either."

"See, if I'd told you, you'da signed up, too. I'm a bad influence on you."

"That's for sure. You've got me in trouble with the Mexicans, and now I'm a tequila smuggler."

"There you go. I rest my case."

"You didn't tell me 'cause you thought I'd follow you?"

"Somethin' like that."

"Fuck you, man. Now who's the pussy?"

"I know you would. You don't want to be a marine."

"You think I'm too pussy to be a marine?"

"Too smart."

Tired and mostly sober now, we said little if anything until we pulled in line to cross the California border, where we knew we'd be asked our citizenship. They'd either pass us through or ask us to pull over so they could inspect the truck.

As we inched closer to the inspection site, I sensed Robert tense.

"Do you think the Mexicans called our border patrol about us?"

"Why would they, and what could they do? Unless they discovered your tequila tank."

"Oh hell. You think they did?"

"Possible, I guess." I tried to sound more worried than I was.

"I'll bet they did. Yeah. That's why they're sending us back. It's a setup."

I sat up straight in my seat. I thought it highly unlikely. The odds the Mexicans knew about the tequila tank and didn't say anything were in our favor, and I felt pretty sure they had no way of contacting our border agents.

But I was pissed.

"Could be. We're about to find out, aren't we … marine?" I put strong emphasis on *marine*.

I felt a strange pleasure in watching Robert sweat out our crossing. He got more fidgety with every forward movement of the truck. When it was our turn, the border patrolman asked our citizenship, where we'd been, and what we'd purchased. Robert pulled it together and said we'd been camping and hadn't purchased anything but a bottle of tequila. The truck was given a once- over, and we were waved through and safe across the border.

"Fuckin' A! We did it, pussy boy." He immediately became his old self.

I sulked, keeping my hurt feelings up for most of the drive back to LA. Why hadn't he told me he'd enlisted? Our dynamics had changed. I felt betrayed somehow.

Once home, Robert started getting ready for Tuesday. I kept realizing my life was about to face a major change with him gone, and I started wishing I had joined the marines with him. When I told him that I was considering joining, he reminded me that it was too late for us to share boot camp together, even if I did enlist.

"Don't be a camp follower. Besides, you're too much of a pussy for the marines." He gave me that look-at-my-perfect-teeth smile and a buddy-jab at my shoulder.

He was right. I was a pussy camp follower. He'd allowed me to be a tagalong friend.

In the days before he left, Robert sold his truck and threw one hell of a farewell tequila party. I watched him work the crowd, truly a person magnet: the kind of guy it felt easy to be around and want around. I noticed he didn't drink as much as usual. He seemed a little off. But when someone would wish him well or raise a bottle or glass to him, he'd yell, "Fuckin' A, man!"

I didn't enjoy the party like the others. The more I drank, the more depressed I got. In the time I'd known Robert, we'd shared big and small together. I began to think of our friendship from a different perspective. I always thought I benefited from our relationship, but he did, too.

He needed someone like me he could call a pussy in order to show he wasn't one. I helped him feel superior because I thought he was. Is that what it amounted to?

Then Tuesday came, and Robert was gone.

I heard from Robert twice while he was at Pendleton boot camp. The second one was a note that he'd graduated and was shipping out. He didn't say where, but I assumed it was Korea.

That was the last I heard from him.

Things were lackluster after that. I had to get a new roommate, Greg, who was OK, but we never got close like I did with Robert. He didn't like to party much and liked his alone time. His indirect influence pushed me toward studying more, and even though I partied with old friends on occasion, my life vibes just weren't right. Another school quarter passed. I turned twenty-one but with little fanfare. Spring break came, and there was no tequila run. But, as they say, life went on.

Then through word of mouth, I heard.

Robert was KIA.

I didn't want to believe it. Guys like Robert didn't die in stupid wars. He was too vibrant, too alive with life. The Big Kahuna. People like me needed people like him. I felt numb, too devastated to accept the truth.

Then I did.

I couldn't tell Robert all that I felt, mostly that I should be grateful he didn't tell me he was joining the marines because I know I would have followed the leader. He was right about that one. He knew me better than I thought.

I decided on a little ceremony in his honor.

I bought a bottle of Jose Cuervo and found a pickup truck in the apartment parking lot. I didn't care whose truck it was; it would do. I dropped the tailgate and sat on it, feet dangling. I opened the bottle of tequila.

"This one's for you, Robert," I said and took a swig.

"This one's for pussy me." I took another.

I raised the bottle in the air.

"Fuckin' A, man."

It was the moment I realized what music can do to people, how it can make you hurt and feel so good all at once.

—Nina LaCour, *Hold Still*

# THE MUSIC MESSIAH

Strong applause hits me as I enter Jake's Place, a small hole-in-the-wall jazz venue. The house lights are dimmed except for the spotlights on the stage area, where it's obvious the musicians have just finished a set. That suits me. It gives me a chance to interview Terry Merlin. Terry can way outplay everyone in this quintet.

The leader gets up from the piano. "Thank you. You're a great audience. The Bill Eden Quintet thanks you so much." Then he points. "The great Terry Merlin on tenor."

Terry barely lifts his eyes to the audience, seemingly unreceptive to the strong rise in applause and whistles for him.

Eden frowns slightly, then points. "Clark Tannen on trumpet." Continued applause. Clark smiles, raises his horn, and bows. Bill points again. "Charlee Harris on bass."

The applause drops a bit but continues as Charlee smiles and waves her bow.

"And Frisco Jones on drums." Frisco thumps a little riff on the drums and waves his sticks.

Calling out over the applause, "And I'm Bill Eden. Thanks for coming. We do one more set. And don't forget to buy our new CD, *Carefree.*"

The scattered clapping fades as the players wave and leave the stage and disperse into the audience as chatter takes over. I miss where Terry disappeared, but I see Eden head to the bar, so I weave toward him through a tight maze of occupied tables.

"Club soda," I hear Bill say to the bartender as I approach. Then he sees me and nods.

"Hey, Wes, what's goin'?"

"Nothing much progressing."

"Whaja think of the set?"

"Just walked in. I'll catch the next one."

"Like to have your opinion. Orally rather than written … unless we knock you out." "How can you go wrong with Terry up there?"

"Yeah. He's what brings 'em in."

The bartender brings Bill's drink. I ask for a beer.

"I'd like to interview him. Cover story for the magazine."

"Good luck with that."

"Why?"

Bill shrugs, hesitates, sips his drink. "He's not what you could call outgoing."

"Meaning?"

"He's a real loner. He's not overly friendly. I mean, we play together OK, but that's it. He doesn't hang with us."

"What's that say about you guys?"

"Duh. Thanks for the compliment."

"Just kidding, man."

He takes another sip.

"Nah. We try. We do. But, like, he comes in for rehearsal, we make our plays, then he leaves. When it's time for the show, he comes in, goes onstage, plays, and leaves when it's all over. Even disappears during breaks. Look around. See him anywhere?"

I did and didn't see him anywhere.

"It's not like he's a prima donna. I mean, we work well together. He takes suggestions, not that he needs many, and we gladly take his. He lets the group strut their stuff, doesn't hog. It's like he's all music, and it ends there, ya dig? We learn from him. I'm the first to admit, he's the man. No complaint there. We're lucky he chose us for whatever his reasons."

"No offense, but why is he playing here? I mean, he's probably—
no, he is the greatest jazz tenor player living. He has and could be
playing with the best cats in the business."

"Yeah. No offense taken. You're right. He's an interesting story."

"So let's hear it."

"Can't. Time for the next set. Hang and I'll fill you in. And I'll
see if Terry will talk to you."

Eden finishes his drink and heads to the stage, and I see the rest
of the band emerge from various places, all but Terry. Then, like he
came from nowhere, there he is with the rest of the quintet. They
settle into place, house lights dim, and the audience quiets down.
Bill snaps his fingers signaling 4/4 time, and the familiar sounds of
"Green Dolphin Street" fill the room.

The group plays well together. They create a comfortable sound
worth listening to, but— how shall I say this—not special? No,
that's too harsh. They're good. As each one of them does their
solos, they prove their melodic competency. But when Terry plays,
well, you feel his duende, that inexplicable feeling of power and
spiritual passion that goes beyond the music itself and digs into
your very being.

Why is he playing here at Jake's Place when he could play any
famous venue in the world for real money?

I listen through their last set and enjoy their arrangements of
mostly standards. They really wail on Dizzy's "Caravan." Frisco hits
the skins like he wants to punch holes in them, and Charlee is no
slouch on the bass. Bill and Clark do a sweet counterpoint that
works. But when Terry plays … well, he has what the business calls
unbelievable chops.

After the set, Bill chats a bit with some people, then joins me at
a table I've taken. Jake's begins to clear out.

"Terry says he's sorry, but he can't stay for the interview tonight."

"Real mystery man, huh?" I feel slighted.

"It's more simple than mysterious."

"So fill me in."

"He's as ethereal as his playing."

"How so?"

"Mind if I join you guys?"

"Hey, Charlee, sit yourself down."

"Thanks." She sits down with a drink in hand.

Charlee, this is Wes Thornhill."

"Nice to meet you."

"Same here. Enjoyed your playing. You could almost hide behind that big bass."

"Thanks. Yeah, sometimes I feel like I'm wrestling that thing. I have to stretch."

"You get your licks in."

"Wes is a music critic."

"Cool. You checkin' us out?"

"Actually, I was hoping to interview Terry."

"Ah, of course."

"Doesn't look like it will happen. Not tonight, anyway."

"Yeah. He's not much of a talker."

"Bill was about to give me some background on Terry."

"You want me to leave, Bill?'

"No. Stay. You can add to what I know."

"So? What have you got?"

"You know he struggled with drugs a while back."

"Yeah. Rumor has it he's clean now."

Bill finished his drink. "He is. At least I think so. I've seen no signs he's usin'."

"Me neither." Charlee traces her finger around the moisture left from the bottom of her glass. "Not since he's been playin' with us, anyway."

"Terry came to me about two weeks ago and said he heard I needed a horn for the group.

I almost flipped out when he said he wanted to join us. I mean, the guy disappeared from the music scene when he was at the top, you know? It's been years since he's recorded or played with anybody. I wanted to ask him where he's been and why us, you know? But I didn't. I just said, "Hell, yes." I told him what we're making, a lot less than he could get, but he accepted it. Said all he wanted was that we time one of our breaks at exactly ten-thirty every night. Seemed odd, but I agreed. Then I worried he might not fit in. I mean, he's the best. How's he gonna handle playin' at our level? We're still lookin' for our sound as a group. But he slipped right in. Gives us positive advice with our arrangements."

"He never told you why he wanted to play with you or why the break at ten-thirty?"

"Naw. But I heard around that he's been living in some Zen monastery for the last four years."

"I'd heard that, too."

"My guess is he went there to get clean. Now he's out, he's probably starting to get back in the game shedding up with us. That might explain why he goes off by himself. He's used to a quiet monastery life. Probably meditates."

"Maybe. But was it just drugs that led him to the Zen thing?"

"There was a woman …"

"What do you know, Charlee?"

"I heard there was this famous singer-actress he was once involved with … you know… Mia Harper?"

"Oh right. I remember. They were a number for a while. Surprised a lot of people."

"Did she dump him?"

"It's what I heard. Devastated him. He was heavy into heroin, and she didn't like it. Gave him a choice. Her or the drugs. I heard he tried but couldn't stay steady, so bye-bye Mia."

"Hence the monastery."

"Not right away. He'd clean up, do some recording, then lose it again. He was tourin' in Europe with—I forget which group—when he got beat up real bad. By some drug dealers, they think. Lost some teeth. Had trouble playing after that."

We all sit in silence for a minute. I turn back to Charlee.

"You know quite a bit about Terry. Maybe you should write my article."

"Funny man. No, mostly hearsay. I've admired him since I was in school. Terry was a legend at Julliard. I mean, he is a legend, you know?"

"For damn sure."

"Sax supreme."

"When he first came on board with us, I guess I gushed over him too much, you know. Maybe he thought I was comin' on to him. He didn't know I was a les then. He may not know now. Anyway, he was nice, but I caught his leave-me-alone vibes."

"You didn't gush. You showed your appreciation for his talent. Anyway, all four of us are still in awe he's playing with us."

"God, I really need to talk to him. I can't write an article about what I'm learning here. I want to discuss his music with him. Verify stuff."

"Come back tomorrow night. Maybe I can get him to talk with you if he knows it's just about his music."

I say my good nights and leave Jake's disappointed. The streets are still busy with people milling about. I decide to walk through the theater district on my way to Smokey's. I know there will be music still going on over there. A lot of musicians go to there after hours to jam. With luck, maybe Terry might be there, though I doubt it after what I heard at Jake's.

As I pass the Gershwin Theater, I notice a crowd hanging outside the stage door. I wonder who they are waiting for. I soon find out. Mia Harper. Funny. We were just talking about her and Terry. I pause and watch the fans seeking autographs and selfies. I wonder if she knows Terry's in town. Would she care? What did they share? Talent, no doubt.

Smokey's is packed. I look around and see famous cats I know but no Terry. I find a stool by the bar and order a beer. I spend maybe an hour listening to some of the greats and lots of wannabes. I decide to pack it in and go home with a head full of musical notes. I dream I'm a musician pounding out clinkers on a piano, trying to find a tag note to end my playing but can't find the right chord. I don't know how to interpret my dream.

The next night, I go back to Jake's Place. I decide I'm going to keep my eyes on Terry and follow him at the break and ask for an interview. Avoiding Bill and the group, I stand by the back exit and wait. At the end of the set, I watch Terry slip through a curtain behind the stage. I do the same, but he's disappeared. Where'd he go? Then I spot him leaving by a door I didn't know was there. I start to catch up with him but decide to follow him instead. I've never stalked anyone before and feel guilty. Not guilty enough to stop following him. Then Terry stops. Why? What's he looking at?

Then I understand. The Gershwin Theater is across the street. I maneuver so I can see. Mia comes out the stage door with another person. They stand there chatting for less than five minutes, then they go back into the theater. Mia's showtime break. Terry stands there for a moment, then he turns and sees me trying to act like I wasn't following him. He throws me off guard.

"We might as well walk back to Jake's together."

"You caught me. I'm sorry."

"You're not very good at following people."

"Yeah. I don't make a habit of it. Sorry."

"Bill tells me you want an interview with me."

"I do. For *UpBeat*. Cover story. I'm feeling so stupid. I'm Wes Thornhill."

"I know who you are. I'll talk to you, but everything is off the record until I give you permission to publish."

"Fair enough."

"After the last session, then."

"Thanks."

We walk back to Jake's in silence.

\* \* \*

I'm anxious during the last set and can't listen like I normally do. I keep thinking of questions to ask Terry. But Terry grabs my attention when he blows "Stella by Starlight." Then Clark picks it up on the trumpet, and I begin to think this group is going to learn and make it.

When the last set ends, I get more anxious. Terry does a disappearing act, and I begin to wonder if he conned me. But after the place empties of customers, Terry shows up from nowhere I could see, and he's sitting next to me at a table.

"I'm beginning to think you can appear and disappear like some sort of spirit." He ignores my comment.

"So what do you want to know?"

"Everything. You. Your music style. You're a musical legend, but lately, you've become... I don't know ... mysterious, mystical ... maybe supernatural to your fans."

"I'm none of those."

"Don't sell yourself short. Fans are curious about your return to the music scene after being gone so long."

"I don't mean to be a mystery."

"So tell me so I can tell your fans."

"We're not on the record yet."

"Understood."

"Where do I start?"

"Let me just say I'm intrigued by what I saw when I followed you. Now I think I know why you want to break at ten-thirty. How did you know Mia took her break at that time? Have you talked with her recently?"

"No. Haven't seen her in years. It was serendipitous. I just happened to be walking by the theater one night and saw her come out. Shook me a bit. Went back the same time the next night, and out she came."

"And you never approached her?"

"Nah."

"May I ask why?"

Terry sighs. Pauses. "Mia and I met at a charity concert about eight or nine years ago. We shared the stage for one act. She has an angel's voice. We did an unplanned number together. It went well. Audience loved it. We hit it off after that, and before we knew it, we were what they call 'an item.'"

Terry pauses again. "Mia's the one you should write about. She has real talent."

"And you don't?"

He smiles and ignores my comment. "Anyway, she became my muse, ya know? My playing improved. I could feel it. So could she. Success came my way. Recordings, gigs, concerts, offers. I got so busy I couldn't keep up. Someone offered me some juice to keep me going. I started bipping. That led to harder stuff. I began to think I was playing better under the influence."

"Were you?"

"Nah. Mia saw what was happening. Gave me an ultimatum. Smack or her. I tried, but I was too far under. I lost reality. So she left me. Told me she was through with me. That I was a weak man who could go right on ruining himself but not around her."

"Must've hurt."

"I became a wreck. But she was right. I wasn't doing her any good. Then in France, I was hanging on, barely, playing with Guy Consitino when I got stomped one night trying to deal with these guys I didn't know, and it was bad, man. Woke up in the hospital. Could barely move.

Broken jaw. Could hardly touch my swollen lips. Lost some teeth."

Terry looks off in space, in remembrance, I'm guessing. Unconsciously shakes his head. "You might say they knocked some sense into me. I couldn't play my horn. Everything fell apart. The hospital staff soon discovered I was an addict, and they helped me some. The doctor told me about this monastery for addicts in southern France. I had no place else to go, and I needed to look at myself and where I was going. Mia was right. So I committed myself."

"For how long?"

"Supposed to be one year."

"But?"

"Four and a half."

"Man, that's some commitment."

"For a while, I thought I'd just stay there … never leave."

"Really."

"Yeah. It was good for me. As my body healed, so did my head and soul."

"In what way?"

"Hard to put into words."

I wait while he gathers his thoughts.

"At the monastery I was exposed to meditation, reading philosophy, exercise, and menial work, all geared toward body and mind cleansing. I discovered I was mostly ego centered, and my views of reality were as narrow as the eye of a needle. I was shown how to lay aside my ego and instead focus on simple tasks so fully that I forgot myself and allowed a new breath of life to enter me. I learned to concentrate so intently on the given job that I can lose ego completely in the task and feel a kind of ecstasy of mind."

"Impressive."

"Not really. It's very basic."

"If you say so. But are you saying that when you play your sax, you kinda go somewhere else?"

"No, not at all. I don't go anywhere. I just become the music. I'm feeling ecstasy."

"You become the music?"

"I don't know any other way of saying it."

"So you don't think about the notes or the timing?"

"Of course I do. It's not easy to explain. I didn't play for two years. It took that long for my mouth and jaw to heal. I was afraid to even try. But in a short time, my playing began to feel different, a new pleasure. My thinking about the notes is almost nonexistent. I feel them more than I play them. I hear the music in the silence between notes. I think I've found the source of artistic inspiration. Something else takes over when I play, and I'm not me; I'm the music itself. Whoa, listen to me."

"I'm not sure I understand what you mean by finding the source of artistic inspiration."

"I'm not, either. I told you; I don't know how to put what I feel into words."

"So what's your direction? I mean, what are your plans?"

"I want to see if I can continue to live in the world and experience what I did in the monastery. Have I really learned anything, or am I kidding myself?"

"Why did you decide to play with Bill's group?"

"This may sound egotistical after just saying I've rid myself of it, but there's talent in Bill's group. I'm hoping I can share what I've learned with them and help them play—no, feel the music with the ecstasy I sense. I think they will understand eventually. I guess I haven't lost all my ego."

"To be frank, they think you're ... well ... cold."

"Good. I want them to be close to the music, not me. I'm not what's important here."

"What happens when you think Bill's group has accomplished what you want to give?"

"I hope other musicians will want to learn."

"No more tours, concerts, recordings, more fame and money?"

"I've done all that, and I see what it does to talent. No. I don't need it. I would only tour and record if I were a part of a group I am working with for their betterment."

"What about your fans? They're going to want to hear from you now that they know you're back."

"I'm not back. I'm on a different train."

Neither of us knows what to say for a time.

"What about Mia? You going to try getting together again?"

"No. She's happy in her life. Why stir up the past? She's always in my heart. My absent muse. But it's too late for the two of us. For me, just looking at her makes me feel steady."

"Shouldn't you let her know your feelings? That you've changed?"

"Why? It wouldn't change anything now. It could mix her up."

"What can I write from all this? I'm not sure I totally understand all you've told me. You sound like some musical spirit."

"Sorry. I can't put it in words. As I talk with you, I realize I sound like I'm contradicting myself, that I'm a music messiah of some kind. But I can't say any of this any better. You're the writer. Think about what I've said. Write something up. Show it to me, and I'll let you know if I'll go or pass on it."

I go home wondering if maybe he is a music messiah. I try to think of an opening line and can't.

\* \* \*

Sleep doesn't help. I struggle to write. I go back to Jake's Place. I want to hear Terry play again, hoping somehow I'll find a lead for my article. The quintet is making their way through "Windmills of Your Mind." They sound different, better, new.

When Terry steps up to play, I close my eyes and really listen. He's no longer up there on a stage but here, in me, sharing the elation he's found.

Grief is not an illness you "get over." Grief is born of love, and you must learn to live with it, moving forward as best you can.

—Beverly Stautzenbach

# TOO LATE, NAYTAN

I've forgotten my travel destination back then, but my flight had been routed through Phoenix. When the flight attendant announced that we should buckle up for our approach to Sky Harbor, some prompt in my brain recalled that Todd, an old high school buddy, lived there or used to. We'd been close friends, but I'd let time and distance get the better of us. This was well before the ubiquitous cell phone, so I decided I'd check a phone book when we landed and give him a long overdue call.

As the plane started its descent, my mind flew backward to the late 1940s in Alton, Illinois, a small town on the Mississippi River. And for me, there's no thinking about Alton without thinking about Todd and how we met.

I remember brown hair cut short, dark eyes, usually dressed in jeans and T-shirt. Todd appeared to be a normal, average-size teenager. That's where it ended. Not the sort to be labeled the most popular boy in the class yearbook, Todd could have cared less if his picture or name appeared in it. As far as I know, he never attended school events or joined any clubs. To most, he was Todd the Odd.

Social skills he had few. Quick to say what he thought, he cared little of its effect on others. He thought nothing of interrupting a conversation to tell someone they didn't know what they were talking about. And they often didn't. Todd's sense of humor was somewhere out there in a zone beyond most of us. He enjoyed an annoying Socratic approach to answering teachers' questions with questions of his own, showing a depth in the subject that often surprised the teachers. My first read on him led me to think he got pleasure from making himself unpopular.

One day in chemistry class, I watched him burn his initials in his forearm with acid.

When I asked why, he said to see what it felt like to be branded like an animal. "Want to try it?" he asked, holding out the bottle of acid.

I shook my head. "Doesn't it hurt?"

He looked at the letter T swelling up on his arm. "Not as bad as it must for a steer." He looked at me. "You think I'm a stupid shit, don't you?"

"It crossed my mind." It came out before I realized I'd said what I was thinking.

"Maybe I am. Who's to say?" He gave a little laugh, and I wondered if he might be trying to impress me with his acid antics.

That was my first conversation with him.

A few days later, Miss Blackard, our history teacher, decided to have the class work in pairs on a project dealing with American presidents. When she assigned Todd and me to write a report on Andrew Jackson, I figured she had it out for me for some reason, and I was being punished. But I resigned myself to the task.

"How do you want to do this?" I asked Todd.

"What do you know about Jackson?"

"Not much. He was president way back and his picture is on the twenty-dollar bill."

"Great start. I see you're going to be an enormous help."

I couldn't think of a smart retort and settled for "Yeah, well, what do you know about him?"

"He was an asshole, for starters."

That threw me. At that age, I'd never heard any of our presidents referred to as assholes.

"What do you mean?"

"Just that. You don't know shit, do you?"

Todd's comments hastened my growing dislike for him and our project. My immediate thought was that maybe if I asked, Miss

Blackard would let me switch with someone else. He didn't appear too eager to work with me, either.

"Look," Todd said, "you research John Marshall and Chief John Ross. Take some notes, and I'll dig up stuff on Jackson. When can you meet to start putting it all together?"

With much reluctance and annoyance at Todd's show-off bossiness, I agreed to his plan and to meet a few days later in the library.

I had no idea who Marshall or Ross were or how they were connected to Andrew Jackson. But once I started reading, I soon learned how Jackson had betrayed them, as well as his part in the brutal treatment of the Indians along the Trail of Tears. I began to see Todd's point.

Andrew Jackson was an asshole.

I surprised myself at both my interest in our project and Todd's knowledge of American history. When I asked him how he knew so much, he just shrugged and said he read a lot.

Miss Blackard accepted our final report, praising us for our research but suggesting our use of language could use some work. I remember our opening line read, "President Andrew Jackson, our seventh president of the United States, was an asshole."

Working together on the Jackson project did not situate us in the best-of-friends category. While I had to admire Todd for his knowledge and accept that he was smarter than I was, I also resented him for those very qualities. Why did he have to act so bizarre? He didn't care what other people thought of him. Me? I did care about my image. Among my friends, not hanging out with him was a given. Yet I envied him in a way I didn't understand at the time. His lack of ordinariness made him interesting to someone like me, a very ordinary teenager. Now, of course, I credit him for opening my mind to ideas and actions I never would have encountered on my own.

Not long after our history project was completed, a group of us gathered at Block's, an ice cream parlor hangout. Todd was there, and we heard him order a Hound Dog without nuts. The server told him a Hound Dog without nuts was just a chocolate ice cream sundae with chocolate syrup.

"Well, that's what I want. A Hound Dog without nuts," he repeated.

"Why don't you just ask for a chocolate sundae?" she asked.

"Because a Hound Dog without nuts is the same thing, isn't it?"

"But if I ring up a Hound Dog, I'll have to charge you for the nuts."

"Why? I don't want the nuts."

She gave Todd a piercing-arrow stare and told him, "I'm fixing you a chocolate sundae.

Take it or leave it."

Someone in the store yelled out, "Way to go! He's already nutty enough."

We all laughed, yet I felt sorry for Todd. Was he trying to be funny and make a joke about a hound dog with no balls? Was he trying to show how ludicrous it was that placing nuts on a chocolate sundae turned it into something called a Hound Dog? I don't know. But I didn't like myself for joining in the laughter directed at him.

Todd paid for his order, saw me, and nodded as he left. I felt sure I saw a slight smile as he dipped his spoon into his Hound Dog without nuts.

One Saturday afternoon, Todd happened to see me at the Grand movie theater. She Wore a *Yellow Ribbon* with John Wayne was playing.

"So, you like westerns." It wasn't a question.

"Good ones." Like I knew the difference.

"Me, too," Todd said. "I like to see how they portray Indians. Half the time, it's some famous white actor with dyed skin speaking in pidgin."

When I thought about other Westerns I'd seen, I realized he was right.

After a newsreel on the progress of the war, a Tom and Jerry cartoon, a travelogue, and some previews of coming attractions, the movie started. Wayne played an army colonel named Nathan Brittle who tried to stop an impending Indian uprising by meeting with an old Indian chief. We noticed that a real Native American played the small part and gave each other a thumbs-up. With tom-toms beating in the background and a fire crackling between them, the Indian elder chief, who seemed to have no teeth, struggled to pronounce Nathan's name, declaring in broken English, "Too … late … Nay-tan … too late."

Todd cracked up at the chief's delivery. I'd never seen him laugh before. But the line stuck with him, and it became a phrase he would use whenever he felt it fit the occasion.

After the movie, we stood around discussing what we liked and didn't like about the movie. We pretty much agreed on everything, which surprised me. It became obvious we both liked many of the movies we'd seen, though he felt the book a movie was based on was better in most cases. I couldn't argue that one. He was better read than I was. I found I enjoyed talking with him, so I shocked myself by asking if he wanted to go to Block's for a Hound Dog.

He smiled and, imitating the chief's scraggy voice, said, "Too late, Nay-tan, too late," then explained he had to get home.

* * *

When the airplane wheels hit the runway, the captain announced that our arrival gate wasn't cleared yet and reminded us to stay seated with seat belts fastened until we were finally gated.

I looked out the window and wondered where in Phoenix Todd lived. There wouldn't be time to visit, but I felt a little excited and a bit nervous about calling. The more I thought about him, the more I realized how much we'd shared as teenagers. I don't know why I hadn't contacted him before. It would have been hard for him to track me down the way I'd moved about. I felt a sting of regret that I hadn't kept in touch.

Our friendship seemed to develop out of nowhere. Little by little, we began hanging out together, doing who remembers what. We both liked to hike up the old gravel river road outside town. I can't count the times Todd and I hiked those railroad tracks north of town, the wide, brown river to our left and the scattered growth embedded in the loosed layered limestone bluffs on the right. They called out to us to be climbed. A Native American pictograph of the mysterious colorful-winged Piasa Bird stood out on the white cliffs just as you left town, supposedly carved originally by the Illini people. Small caves hid themselves in the rugged high bluffs. Our favorite we named Dry Cave.

I've heard all that's gone now, tracks and cliffs blasted away to make way for a paved road and a bicycle path, the mythic bird repainted on one remaining cliff, a loss for kids growing up there today. But back then...

* * *

"Hey, Naytan (by then, that had become my tag), bet I can balance myself on the rails longer than you can," he might challenge, and that would start our hike along the tracks that seemed to merge in the distant shimmering heat waves. "Can you do this?" might come a dare, as he managed some crazy one-leg leap on the rails.

He'd pull stunts like picking up something at his feet and examining it as if it were a world-shaking geological find or ancient artifact, then try to convince me of its scientific importance.

"You should keep this," he'd say, holding out some kind of rock or mud clot.

"Why? What is it?"

"A beautiful specimen."

"Of what?"

He'd shake his head at me. "Your ignorance appalls me, you know that?" Then he'd throw the item away. Or, for no reason, he'd throw it at me, forcing me to retaliate until the rock throwing grew too serious to continue.

About a mile out of town, we'd usually climb the scaly bluffs and find Dry Cave, sit at the entrance, and look out over the river to the Missouri side. The Alton dam formed a huge lake just north of town, so the river was wide and a not-inviting milk chocolate color. Sometimes, tugs would come down river pushing barges, and we'd make up stories about where they came from and where they were going, what they carried, and at what city down the river we'd get off if we were on board, arguing over which offered us the most: Cairo, Memphis, Natchez, Vicksburg, or New Orleans. Our future destinations and plans ran wild, each trying to outdo the other.

I remember he relished looking for snakes. He knew the names of every one he caught. If they weren't poisonous, he'd let them go. But the bluffs were full of copperheads. The way he handled them scared me. He would kill copperheads by cutting off their heads with a four-inch knife he always wore in a sheath attached to his belt. The first time I saw him do this, he held the squirming four-foot body at my face, proud of his prize. I tried hard to conceal my unease; otherwise, who knew how he might play at my fear.

"Let's find out if what they say is true," he said.

"Which is what?" I asked with some apprehension, knowing him.

"Supposedly, a snake's body with its head cut off will keep wiggling until sundown. Let's see if it's true."

He put a rock on top of the severed head, stomped on it, and then carried the body, still squirming, down the bluffs to the railroad. He put the body between the tracks and said, "We'll check on that theory on our way back."

As interesting theory, but I never found out its validity. A slow freight train leaving the city made its way north. We stood back and watched it rattle toward us, its deep horn blaring a warning. The ground shook, and the engineer waved. We watched as car after car rolled by us. I'd never been that close to a moving train before.

"Let's catch it," Todd yelled over the noise, his daring grin showing.

I just looked at him, hoping he was kidding.

"Yeah, why not? It's slow. We can jump off when we want to." Without waiting for me to argue, Todd started running alongside the train.

"You're outta your gourd," I yelled.

I watched as he jumped, grabbed at an iron ladder rung on the side of the boxcar, and pulled himself up. He stepped a couple of rungs up and waved at me.

In a momentary loss of brains, I ran alongside the train. Like Todd, I grabbed a ladder rung on the boxcar and lifted my feet up to the bottom rung just over the train wheel. But as I pulled myself up, my feet slipped off the rung. My chest washboarded down the iron rungs, scraping away skin, and my legs dropped down over the wheel. Something like an electric shock hit one foot, and it flipped way out from the train. Instinct drew my flailing legs back up, and I finally found a rung to rest my feet on. My eyes blurred with tears as my heart sped faster than the train. I stayed in a squatting position, hugging the ladder like a baby monkey holding on to its mother.

When I looked forward at Todd, he was posed like a trapeze artist, one leg out from the train and one arm outstretched, waving to his imaginary crowd. At that moment, I hated him.

Keeping my feet firmly on the ladder rung, I slowly pulled myself up hand over hand to a standing position. Nervous sweat made my hands slippery and holding on difficult. I started feeling the pain in my chest and looked down to see some blood on my torn shirt. More painful would be telling my parents when I got home. If I got home.

But that seemed less significant when I realized the train was gaining speed. I wanted no more of Todd's craziness, but that meant I had to jump or stay on a train going who knew where and for how long.

I looked down at the rail dirt and gravel that seemed to be sailing by and jumped as far out from the train as I could. I tried to keep running once I hit the gravel, but that was a fool's errand. That day, I created the term *rock and roll*. When I stopped rolling on the rocks and scraggly weeds, I lay there, certain I never wanted to move again. I closed my eyes and listened to the steady sound of the train wheels—*alump-udet-alump-udet-alump-udet*—change to you- stupid-boy-you-stupid-boy-you-stupid-boy. But soon all the burning, stinging cuts, scratches, and bruises forced me to sit up and check the damage. Nothing felt broken, but my elbows and knees were a mess. My scraped chest carried scars for years after. It was then I looked at my feet and noticed my sock was sticking out the sliced-off tip of one of my shoes.

Todd limped toward me, checking out a bleeding cut on his arm. He looked at me down on the ground and grinned.

"We jumped too late, eh, Naytan?"

Naytan bombarded him with curses and rocks.

\* \* \*

Finally, the plane began its slow move again toward our assigned gate and ended my reverie. After another short forever, we single filed into the terminal. I found a phone stall near the gate, but it was in use. I checked the departure screen and noted that my connection was only a few gates away.

While waiting for the phone, I remembered that, in the winter of our senior year, we went ice-skating on the small lake in the country club golf course. Neither of us had ever ice-skated before, but Todd somehow came up with a pair of skates for both of us. He took to it pretty quickly, but my ankles wanted to do most of the skating, so I clunked around, searching for balance until the ice cracked, then broke, and I went in to my neck.

In shock, I floundered in the frigid water, trying to find something solid to grab, but the more I flailed, the more the ice around me splintered. I felt the weight of the skates and the wet winter clothes pulling me down. I kicked in panic at nothing, causing me to bob up and down, my heavy, flying arms searching for support. I'd lost control and felt the strength of fear.

"Quit moving!" Todd yelled. "Grab my sleeve!" He had taken off his coat, held one sleeve, and threw the other at me. He lay on his stomach on what must have been more solid ice near the edge of the lake.

"I can't reach it," I sputtered, growing more panicked.

He edged closer to me, and to this day, I don't know why the ice didn't break under him.

He tossed the sleeve at me again, and I grabbed it. Todd told me to be still and began slowly pulling me closer until I was able, with his help, to pull myself up on a more solid ice patch. At least, that's how I think it went down. When frightened out of your wits, as I was, memory can play tricks.

Did I thank him or blame him for that one? I don't remember. What I do remember him saying with that grin of his was, "Almost too late, eh, Naytan?"

Once the terminal phone was free, I checked the local telephone directory and found Todd listed, which made me feel a touch of guilt. Why hadn't I called before this convenient stopover? I hesitated before dialing, wondering what Todd remembered about me. Anyway, I decided it would be fun to jog his memory a bit and remind him how he saved "Naytan" many years ago.

As the phone rang, I grew anxious. Some small part of me wanted no one to answer.

What had Todd's life been like these past twenty-odd years? Were my memories his? It had been so long. After graduation, Todd went to Texas to work on a rattlesnake farm, milking them for their venom. When summer was over, we went our separate ways to college. In 1951, both back home during a sophomore semester break, we got together for our last hike up the river. Mostly, we bragged about girls we'd met, talked about how different college was from high school, the influence of the books we were reading. At that time, we both felt akin to Sartre and existentialism. Was God dead? Was God ever alive? Was God male or female? What was consciousness? Were the bluffs we sat on, the river below us, real? Were the two of us seeing everything as identical images? How grown up I felt discussing ideas college had planted in our heads.

But then we broached the Korean conflict and the country's fight against communism, which we really didn't understand. What we did understand was the fact that we would be drafted soon. Neither of us liked the idea of going into the army, not from what we saw in newsreels and war movies. For a while, we sat in silence, wondering what our futures held. I watched the quiet, drifting, gray-brown water below, aware that this might be the last time would share our river adventures.

"Do you think you could kill someone—I mean, like, in a war?"

"I guess if I had to. Before they killed me, I'd hope." I'd never asked myself that question before.

"Imagine yourself in Korea. A Korean or Chinese soldier is coming at you, firing away. Does preservation take over? Is it automatic to shoot back? Would you freeze in fear? Do you think about the fact you're killing someone?"

"We'd get training for that, wouldn't we?"

"Yeah. Training to kill. Think about that. We're taught that 'Thou shalt not kill' here at home. Yet we do kill. We give the death penalty to people who murder. We go in the army, and they teach us how to kill. Why isn't that called murder?"

"I don't think you can call it murder when you kill someone who is trying to kill you."

"OK, let's just call it 'taking a life.' When is it OK to take someone's life?"

"In war. Our enemies want to kill us, so we try to kill them first." I was beginning to doubt the simplicity of my words.

"War's really stupid, you know. Our so-called enemies are trained to kill us; we're trained to kill them. They probably don't want to fight any more than we do. But our politicians and generals, who never have to do the dirty work, tell guys like us to line up, be patriotic, and kill some enemy who has been told by their politicians and generals to kill us. Whichever side has the most guys standing after the shooting wins. And we don't get a choice. Not really. You're labeled a coward or unpatriotic if you don't fight. But what have all the poor dead guys on either side won when it's all over?"

"I think it's more complicated than that."

I didn't really know what I was talking about, but it had to be more complex than Todd's description. Yet his simplistic explanation made some sense to me.

"When they teach thou shalt not kill, they should put an asterisk at the end." That sent us both into silence for a time.

Todd broke the quiet, shouting at the river. "Screw the army, Naytan! Korea's a land war.

Let's join the navy before the army makes us gun fodder."

And just as I'd jumped on that train with him, I jumped on Todd's idea, and the next day, we joined the navy.

We got split up in boot camp. During our four years in the service, we saw each other once or twice on leave. Todd was right. Neither one of us got close to Korea. After being discharged, we again went our separate ways. The last time I saw him was after we had graduated from our respective colleges, and, by chance, we were both back in Alton. He had married and invited me to a family dinner party before leaving on his honeymoon. I met his wife, Ann, and Todd introduced me as his old friend Naytan. That was 1960. Many lifetimes ago.

\* \* \*

"Hello." A scratchy woman's voice brought me up short.

"Oh hi." I cleared my own voice. "Is Todd there?" Feeling foolish I hadn't asked if the voice was Ann's.

The voice became guarded. "Who's this?"

"Is this Ann?" I asked, trying to sound upbeat.

"Yes, who's this?"

I told her. "I don't know if you remember, Ann. We met at your honeymoon dinner."

Her breath came in gasps. "Yes … yes, I remember."

"I'm out at the airport. Had a stopover and thought I'd call and see how you and Todd were doing. It's been so long. Is Todd there?"

There was a slight pause.

"Todd's … dead. More than two years now." Her voice wheezed.

A hand reached into me and squeezed my heart.

Too thrown to grasp everything that was said between us, I learned that he had had a heart attack, that they had two adult children still living in Phoenix, and that Todd had tried to contact me over the years. Ann suffered from asthma and didn't sound healthy. It turned into an awkward, unfulfilled conversation.

I do remember she said Todd had valued our friendship, talked about me often. I repeated my condolences, and we said goodbye. But just before I took the phone from my ear to hang up, I was sure I heard "Too late, Nay-tan. Too late."

Hatred is an affair of the heart;
contempt that of the head.

—Arthur Schopenhauer

# EVER AFTER

"Please go see her. She wants to see you."

"Why? I haven't seen her or talked to her for nearly twenty years."

"She's dying."

I knew it, of course. My oldest son informed me the end was near. By emphasizing the word *dying*, was he trying to pressure me into an untenable position? His mother, my ex-wife, lay dying in the hospital of pancreatic cancer and pneumonia complications.

I couldn't come out and tell him that I couldn't care less, but in truth, I didn't care. Call me heartless, but a part of me saw her death as the period that goes at the end of a tough sentence, a twenty-two-year sentence spent with her. Discussing her death made for an unwanted interruption of my present life. For thirty-five years now, I've been living a fulfilling, contented life with my second wife, the clearest and most fortunate years of my long life. Now I was being asked to return to an era I didn't care to enter again, an intrusion into my present comfort zone. I had nothing to say to her and nothing I wanted to hear from her.

"Please," my son said. "Why can't you just go visit, see what she wants to say? Why are you resistant?"

Ah, if you only knew, I wanted to say. But I held in my long-contained malice and could see it was important to my son that I go.

I relented.

When I got to her hospital room, my son and two daughters stood by her bed, but they decided to leave their mother and me alone and left. The cold room evoked hospital discomfort with its excessively sweet smell of flowers mixed with unavoidable medicinal odors, and the monotonous monitor beeping through the silence brought back unwanted memories of my own history of hospital stays. With some resentment and misgivings, I approached my ex alone for the first time in years. I guess I was expecting her to look as I remembered her, so it took me a moment to realize time and illness had diminished her physically. Sometimes I forget that she and I are in our eighties. Her usually tanned skin now pale and chalky, her dark hair now gray and sparse, set me back for a moment. Her closed eyes made me think that maybe she didn't want to see me either, that my son had set us up. She was just being stubborn and pretending to sleep as a way to ignore me.

I felt my jaws clinch. "You wanted to see me?" I sounded as cold as the room, even to me.

She didn't respond.

"Sam said you wanted to see me."

Still no response.

I moved closer and looked down at the woman with whom I had spent over twenty years of my life, and, despite her condition, I couldn't suppress the resentment I thought had dissipated over the years.

You're still manipulating us, right up to the end, aren't you? Using the kids to get me here.

Just like you.

Well, I'm here. Speak your piece.

Nothing to say?

Well, I do.

Why did I wait so long to leave you?

Well, that part's not really your fault. I trapped myself. I take full credit. It's ironic, isn't it?

Here we are in a hospital again, you lying in bed, wanting to tell me something.

Remember what you told me that first year we were married, on the eve of our first child being born? It's still vivid to me. You were in the naval hospital in Portsmouth, and I'd been granted shore leave to be with you. You were all prepped, and your contractions were starting. The doctors were going to make me leave once the baby started coming. You took me by surprise and began crying. I felt unsure of myself, sympathetic, nervous, so useless: a twenty-two-year-old sailor, newly married and on the verge of fatherhood, not yet even broken in as a husband. I had no idea how to comfort you. I'd never seen you cry before, and I didn't know how to react, so I asked …

"Is the pain bad?"

"Un-huh, when the contractions come. But it's … it's not that."

"What is it?"

"I … I know I should have told you before."

"What?"

"I'm afraid to have the baby."

"Why? I mean, so am I, but the doctor said everything looked OK."

"He doesn't know."

"Doesn't know what? What should he know? What are you talking about? What does it have to do with having a baby?"

"I should have told you before. I'm sorry."

"Tell me now."

You turned your head from me.

"It was before I met you. I've had … I know I should've said something … I had … two abortions before I met you."

One of those "Wait, what?" shock moments that can leave the brain confused as it tries to filter the information while part of you wants to flee to the far side of another time.

You sobbed out, "I'm afraid there might be internal damage or that something could go wrong."

I went numb with the unexpected. What was she saying? What was I expected to do with this information?

But you didn't stop there.

"There's more."

I didn't want to hear more. I hadn't processed what you'd said about abortions.

"I've done drugs." More tears. "Heroin."

"Jesus." My mind groped for control like one gropes for the surface when drowning; my naïve heart felt knifed by your confession. Who were you? What? What is all this?

"It was all before I met you. I quit, long time ago. I'm sorry I didn't tell you before, but—"

Before I could digest this disturbing, upending, unwanted news, an overly cheerful doctor and a nurse came and chased me out of the room, assuring me everything was going to be fine but leaving me in need of a help-me-out-here sedative.

They wheeled you away, leaving me with an exploding, fragmented brain bomb.

What was I to do with all you just told me?

The waiting room at the naval hospital was lacking comfortable furniture and full of sailors like me waiting in various stages of anticipation for our wives to give birth. A loudspeaker in the upper corner of the room announced the name of the father when his child was born and told the cubicle number assigned to the mother and baby. The smiles and happy faces of those whose names were called out conflicted with the swirling turmoil inside me. My thoughts zigged and zagged, went far and wide, creating a sense of anger, not knowing how to process what you told me. I felt lied to, yet you'd just told me the truth, a truth I didn't want to hear. You suddenly weren't the same person I thought I'd married. I wanted to walk out the hospital door and leave you and all you had told me behind. I wanted to tell you to forget having a baby; I didn't want one now; I wanted to start a new life. I wanted to yell at you for making me feel like such a fool for marrying someone who had had two—two—abortions, leaving me with back-room coat-hanger images. I hated you, felt jealous of your apparently having had sex with several different men, even if it might have been only one. You did drugs. God, I didn't even smoke. Oh, the images, the images. Who were you really? What else did you have to tell me that was going to rip me further apart?

I should have listened to my dad. When I called my parents and told them I was getting married, he said don't do it. You'll never finish college when you get out of the navy. You're too young. You're lonely and needy right now. You've only known the girl for a few months. You'll be at sea for another year. What are you thinking?

He was so right. What was I thinking? I didn't need to rush into marriage just because I had orders to ship out. You would have waited for me to be discharged if you really cared about me. And would I have cared about you after a year had gone by? I rushed you into this. I can't blame you for that. I didn't want to let you go. I thought I was experiencing love. It didn't take too long for me to realize it was lust. You were my first real sex partner, so much more experienced than I was. Now I know why.

Well, at least you told me. You must have gone through your own hell right then, I imagine, wondering how I was going to respond to what you told me, wondering if the baby would be healthy, whether or not you were going to have birthing complications. You'd been in Portsmouth, alone, when I was at sea, away from your family and friends. Now you'd be alone with a baby when I was gone. And you didn't really know me any more than I knew you. You had your side of the coin, your own unease. That didn't excuse you, though. Would it have made any difference if you'd told me before? I don't know. Who can tell now?

It's all done. As my dad would tell me, "You made your bed, now lie in it." And I did, even as the bed got lumpier over the years.

Strange, isn't it? After the baby was born, I never brought up what you told me that night.

I never confronted you with it. Why? I don't know. You never did, either. I tucked it away somewhere, managed to subdue it, because I guess I didn't want to confront it or even acknowledge it or know what it all meant at the time. In retrospect, I should have. Instead, I let it fester. But you and the baby were healthy, we survived the navy, and we settled into a '50s lifestyle. I worked, finished my degrees, and managed to find a teaching job. We raised five children, and all seemed normal on the surface.

I excused your tendency to flirt with my male friends. But as the girls got older, even to their annoyance, you'd flirt with their boyfriends as if you were jealous of them. You wanted attention. Then you began those periodic disappearances and late nights you pulled on me when you claimed you'd gone to a movie or a friend's, both of us knowing full well you lied no matter how much I pushed for the truth. I admit I didn't think too much about your drinking until it became excessive, and your affair with a grade school principal came to light. You claimed it never happened, but the truth came out. When you started blacking out and not remembering what happened when you drank, I tried to get you to seek help, but you refused to acknowledge your problem even after you totaled the car.

I lived with your excuses and recklessness so long it all became a habit, a way of life, always hoping you'd change. Why did I ignore your actions? Why did I live a numb existence? The tipping point should have come after my office mate confessed you'd come on to him, but the ultimate betrayal was your drunken affair with Bob, my then–best friend. I doubt that I'll ever forgive the hurt and pain caused by the betrayal of you both. That was the end for me.

I've asked myself—in fact, I'm still asking—why I tolerated your behavior for so long. Love? I wonder now if there really ever was any. What was I holding on to? Was it a sense that marriage is for better or for worse? Possibly. Because of the kids? Certainly, in part. I was raised as a good midwestern Methodist. Was I in denial? Maybe denial that I was not giving you what you wanted. Maybe denial of my own unhappiness. My enjoyment and the sense of worth I received from attending and finishing college, loving teaching, connecting with students. Or was it shame? Maybe. It's possible I didn't want to admit I'd made a mistake marrying you, avoiding what leaving you would entail. I did hope you'd change, but I finally gave up on that. I did wait until our children were older before it struck me I wanted something better for myself. I remember you told our kids I was not just divorcing you. I was divorcing them, too. How like you. I could have told them about you. But I didn't, and so for a while, they were on your side.

I have my faults, too. Maybe your actions were a way of asking for something I couldn't give, something I lacked in order to give you more happiness. I see now you were living a sham marriage just as I was, neither of us admitting it. You must have wanted more, too. I failed to look at the causes of your behavior, your seeming need to test me with your actions. During those early years of lousy teacher pay, in order to make ends meet, I had to teach summer school and night classes, even take a part-time job selling insurance. There was never enough time for family or me or, I guess, you. Circumstances absorbed the time I'd rather have spent being a better husband and father. But even if I had, would you have been there? Would we have paid more attention to each other?

I looked at her again and started to say goodbye, but I knew by then she was not pretending. A momentary wave of pity and sorrow washed over me, but I wasn't sure if it was for her or for me. I left wondering why I came.

A few days later one of my daughters called.

"She's gone, Dad. This morning."

I tried to feel what she must be feeling, but it wasn't in my reach.

You will soon discover that in matters of the heart, memories are much kinder than reality.

—Judith McNaught

# SCAR SONG

I should have known.
Obvious now.
Like looking in a rearview mirror ...

When you mailed me your worn-down Chet Baker albums.

Then you sent me the '50 Mercury model car I gave you years ago.
I emailed you:
What's up, bro? Kissing me off?
Joke.
No answer.

I should have asked more.
Should have phoned.
Should haves.

And then came that faded red entrance ticket from Peacock Alley.
That's the night I sneaked underage you to see Chet.
Nothing else in the envelope ... no note ... nothing.
Over fifty years.
You kept that ticket for over fifty years ... fifty years ...
Then the call.

Only a few weeks to live.

The main words I heard from your wife.
Only a few weeks to live.
Other words sunk in later.
Breast cancer.
My brother has breast cancer.
Wait, men can get breast cancer?
Only weeks to live.
What the fuck?

How do I handle that?
Why wasn't I told?
Why wasn't I told sooner, Felicia?
 It's what he wanted.
The hell with what he wanted. You should have told me.
He sent you things.
You might have read something was wrong.
Read them? You make it sound like his dying is a game.
What can I say? It's what he wanted.

What he wanted … what he wanted …You should have told me,
dammit.

Let's not argue. This is hard on me. It's not been easy dealing with
this alone.
I know … sorry. You just knocked me off my center. If only …
He's stubborn.
Always has been.
Ah, Christ.

I'll fly out tomorrow first plane I can get.

You won't recognize him. He fades in and out … morphine.
Nothing you can do.
Can I talk to him now?
It's hard for him. Can I call you back when he's awake?

Don't bother. I want to be there. I'm coming. I'll call you when I
get in.

# SCAR SONG

*  *  *

Brother, brother, brother. Not the way to bring me up to date.
When did we last see each other?
Vegas.

About two years ago.

Can't believe it's been that long.

We met there pretty frequently. You came over for business
conferences every year.
You loved the slots. Tried to get you to play craps with me, but you'd
rather watch.
You seemed healthy then.
Breast cancer ... no ...

You can't go before me, little brother. Hang in there ... I'm coming.
The shits ... why didn't we stay in closer touch?
My fault, your fault—that's us, though, isn't it?

When I had my operation, you were Johnny-on-the-spot. Right
there with me.
You know I'd have been there for you if you'd told me sooner. I don't
understand.
I'm remembering when you had that car accident.

Sixteen, you were.

The police called—you'd smashed up Dad's car. They didn't say
how bad you were hurt.
I rushed to the hospital, worried sick.

You there in bed, unconscious—tubes, monitors, drips ... We
thought we were going to lose you.
You lost those two front teeth ...

*  *  *

57

When you were small, we called you Little Pear because of your chubby shape. You were inquisitive and into everything. Back then, you were just my kid brother, and I led a different life, having eight years on you. But as you got older, we connected more, and you seemed vulnerable, and I felt the need to take care of you. Like the time we were snow sledding. I came down the hill on my sled, and some kid was trying to take yours. I shoved him away from you and gave him what for. And that time you came home from grade school crying because someone said you walked like a duck. Well, you did a little. You hadn't lost your pear shape yet. I taught you to sing, "Be kind to your fine feathered friends, 'cause this duck has a very big brother" to the tune of "Stars and Stripes Forever." We practiced singing it together, and the deal was you would sing it to this jerk who was bothering you. But you were too afraid or shy or whatever. So I met you after school one day, and we found this kid, and I stood behind you while you sang him our ditty in your soprano voice. While you sang, I stared at this guy with the most menacing look I could muster. He never bothered you again. I wasn't tough, just bigger. But you were impressed. Then you surprised us when you lost that pear shape and grew into a beanpole.

By the time you were sixteen, you'd filled out and become one handsome kid. When I got back from the army, I hardly recognized you. I remember you were taken with my wristwatch, so I gave it to you, and you acted like you'd won the lottery. It made me feel like a big brother. But we got closer when you started working for me after school. I used the money I'd saved during my service and opened an automobile trim shop, applying some of my learned skills. Started out slow, mostly seat covers and then headliners, door panels, floor mats, convertible tops, things like that. Cars were easier to work on in those days. Everybody wanted seat covers in their cars. I hired one other worker, and you caught on quickly. Business wasn't bad, except in winter. Sometimes we'd get no customers at all, and we'd watch westerns on the store's TV. Or we'd sing pop songs along with the radio. We knew most of them. You were good at harmony. We were a pretty good duet. We really mastered "Now Is the Hour," as I recall. One winter day, business sucked, and you called a radio station DJ and told him to play "Spring Is Here," and he laughed when you told him we needed business. Surprised, he gave us a free ad on the spot. Later, he brought in his convertible for a new top. And there's that day we both still marvel about. I drove you home in a rain that was pounding like bullets on the car. We sat there waiting for it to lessen, when the music in the car welled up as if in competition with the rain, and we were overtaken by Ravel's *Daphnis and Chloe*. We'd never heard it before, but my Studebaker Starlight coupe became our little pod from the outside weather and put us in some kind of spell we shared without speaking. I think that's when you really started appreciating music. When a new album of Baker came out, I was on it. You'd come to my place, and we'd put the new record on my high-fidelity Magnavox and play it over and over, then compare it to his other albums. I'll never forget your excitement that night I got you in to see Chet's quartet. I didn't need that ticket to remember. You grew up while I wasn't paying attention. By the time you graduated high school, you had enough money to buy that '50 Mercury. You did so much tuck-and-roll upholstery in that car it felt like a padded cell. But your girlfriends loved it. Especially that Swedish student staying with our parents. She taught you a trick or two, as I recall. I was jealous.

\* \* \*

Is he sleeping?

Yes. He knows you're coming and tried to stay awake, but he tires quickly.
I would have come sooner if I'd known.
I know … I wanted to call you ages ago, but he made me promise not to.
Why?
I don't know. It's bothered me. I knew you would want to know, but he insisted.
I know it's been hard on you. Sorry you had to carry the brunt of this.
Horrible. Miserable. Watching him fade away. The hospice people have been wonderful.
Good doctors?

Yes. But he wouldn't listen until it was too late. He kept trying
Eastern medicines.
Why?
I think he was afraid of having surgery and hoped he could fight
the cancer other ways.
Maybe because of our dad. He died during his cancer surgery.
I know. I'm sure that's part of it.

He's always been stubborn on some things.

Ha. Tell me about it
You won't recognize him. He's so thin. Body almost skeletal.
Just wisps of hair left.

He had great hair. Will he recognize me?

It may take a minute, but he's been waiting for you. He will.
Two weeks?
Or less.

I just can't grasp it …

\* \* \*

Strange … I don't recognize you.

You already look dead lying there.
Pear, oh Pear.
Gone that handsome man.
Are you that man?
Why didn't you listen to the doctors?

You were the first in the family to get a college degree.
You did well for yourself.
And now …

Once again, sitting beside your bed, but no hope this time …

\* \* \*

# SCAR SONG

I'm not good with death ...

Is anybody? I don't know.
I know I had problems with both Mom and Dad dying.
Something in me buckled ... on both occasions.
You took over and made the arrangements.

Maybe it's because you where there, and I was across the country.

But even when I arrived, you stayed in charge ... took care of everything. I felt like an outsider.
You became the big brother for the family.

And it was fine with me ... although I felt worthless ... shamed even. But you'd become quite the successful take-charge man. On your own, you developed a thriving insurance business.
With your looks and voice, you could sell life insurance to a dead man.
Not a good analogy.
You no longer needed me ...

\* \* \*

Hey, looks who's awake.
Yeah, it's me, bro.
You came.
Of course. Why would you think otherwise?
Where's Felicia?
She left us alone for a bit.
I'm dying.
Sorry.

She's ... been great ... hard on her.... . Always been ... the good wife.
You're lucky to have her.
Thanks ... for coming.

Why thank me? I should've been here sooner; you didn't ...
Yeah, yeah, yeah.

Why so secretive?

What? I didn't ... catch that.
We didn't need to ...
What ... keep in touch? Yes, we did. We did ... when it counted.
Not this time. Damn, bro.
Drop it ... OK ... change subject ...
Fine. But I'm still pissed at you.
Ha ... our parents ... loving ... weren't they?
Ever so. The best.
They ... taught us well. Except to stay in contact better.
Right from wrong ... love ... kindness ...

Are you having trouble talking? Wanna stop? Rest?
Yeah ... hurts a bit ... but no ...
Thinking a lot about ... Mom and Dad... . Wonder if I'll ... see
them soon ...
Never know.
You don't ... believe it ...

I don't know what to believe, so I don't believe in anything.
Never thought ... I did.
Wishful thinking ... I guess.
Whatever happens in the after, you won't be goin' anyplace bad.
You were ... good brother.

Were? Hope I still am.

I'd smile ... but it ... hurts.
Frown, then.
I know ... I'm dying.

Ah now ...

You saved me, you know. From what? When?
The river ...

The river? Oh, you mean when Dad threw you in and said swim.

Could've drowned ... but you jumped in.

Dad wouldn't have let you drown.
Scared me.
You did OK.

Only 'cause … you were there…with me.

It's the way he learned to swim. Me, too.
Still hate swimming.
You swam pretty fast when we saw that shark.

Scared me…. You, too…. Last time     in the water.

That's a shame, with all this water around you.
Yeah, well …
You gave me…your bike.

You're going way back now. I wasn't using it much anymore then.
You taught me…how to ride.

Believe me, it wasn't easy.
Skippy … remember …
Ah, how could I forget? Mom got all over you. No dogs, she said.
He needed a home…. Followed me … from school.
She said no, but you stuck to your guns. She finally loved that dog
more than us.
Not very … bright, though.
Finally, you admit it.
Couldn't teach him shit … But he was loveable.
You know … what my … best job was?
What?
Working with you … at your shop.

Yeah, it was fun. You were a good worker.

Would've stayed … but Dad … wanted me … go to college.
Rightly so. You aced high school.
You should have gone.

Not me. Some of us aren't suited for college.
Bull.

I'm a hands-on person. You're a brain person. You made the folks proud and me.

Things good…at the shop?

Cars are more difficult to work on. I have three employees now, none like you.

Like Chet sang … there will never be … another you …
That's about the size of it.

Still … into … Chet?

Sometimes, yeah. After he died, some new stuff came out… Sad ending.

What… happened?

He fell out a window. Probably on drugs. Some think he was pushed.
I had … Felicia … send you    my records.
I got them, thanks. And the Merc model. Lots of memories there.

Will you … help Felicia?

Any way I can.,

She won't … need to … worry 'bout … finances…. Arrangements made…
Good.
Sorry 'bout Beverly.

It's for the best. Bev needs more stimulation than I can give her. Fact is I'm pretty boring.
Not … the bro I know.
You know I'm not very gregarious, not a party guy. She's more outgoing.

She let…a…good guy…go.

Debatable. You weren't married to me.
Get to Vegas…much?
Haven't been since our last get-together.
Long…time.
No reason to go anymore. Expensive, too.

What about…playing craps? You…love it.

Only when you watch me.

Never … caught on…. The game's…too fast.

You're better for it.

Lot of … crazy dreams … thoughts … these meds …
Yeah?
Saw … Mom and Dad … dancing … dressed like … for Eastern
Star stuff.
Really?
Yeah…. They smiled … waved … waved to me.
Nice image.
Bro … I'm dying.

What can I say to that?

I'm scared.

I would be, too.

Who would've … thought … breast cancer … would bring me …
down?
You're handling it well.
Not always … ask Felicia…You'll help her?

Count on it.

She bought … *Daphnis and Chloe* for me…. Plays when…pain bad.

Always be special to me, too. We used … to sing together.
Yeah, we gave it a what for.

Hey, you OK? Can I get you something?
I ... I ... let's sing.
What?

Sing ... like we used to.

I don't know  you OK?

Please...sing...
You started singing.
"Now is the hour ... when we must say ..."

\* \* \*

So I joined your faint, scratchy, tuneless voice ... digging deep for
the lyrics.
Then soon realized...
I was singing alone.

The best and most beautiful things in the world
cannot be seen or even touched – they must be felt
with the heart.

—Helen Keller

# TIES THAT BIND

**"I**'d rather not."

Paul could imagine what they'd done to her.

"Don't be silly. They did a nice job."

Paul saw the tired pain on his father's wrinkled face disappear for a moment, revealing those dark eyes he remembered from his youth that demanded, "I'm your father. Do as I say."

Paul stared back. He wanted to yell, "Nice job? They did 'a nice job'? That's your wife— my mother—you're talking about!"

But the thought was enough as he saw his father's moist eyes fade into swollen redness. Paul added more softly, "Look, I … I just don't want to look. OK? I want to remember her as I last saw her. Can we leave it at that?"

Then his sister Nancy started in. Her usually open, pretty face was puffed, poised to cry some more. "But it's the last time you'll get to see Momma."

Paul tensed. Nine years younger than Paul, she knew a father more settled, more financially secure than in those lean, busy years when their dad struggled to make ends meet. There had been little time for a strong father-son bond, only a few memories of any meaningful togetherness with his dad. No slacker when it came to work, their father earned what he now had. But some of it came at Paul's expense, along with a slight envy of Nancy's relationship with their father.

Paul shook his head. He knew they both meant well, but he was tired of their insistence, tired from the cross-country flight and lack of sleep, tired of everything, really. He wished himself away, anywhere but here at this absurd social event where everyone—people he didn't know, relatives he didn't remember—gave somber hugs and spoke in soft voices, praised his mother—wonderful woman, so sweet, what a loss—she'll be sorely missed—your poor father— oh, how she so missed you and her grandchildren, you way out there in California... .

Paul suspected what they implied had more to do with being distant than distance.

Across the room he saw his wife, Linda, in her new black dress, smiling and nodding along to the conversation with someone he didn't remember, perhaps someone from his parents' church. In all likelihood, she was enjoying all this, the end of her having to deal with his mother. Behind her, in contrast, his daughter, Laura, now a young woman he suddenly realized, sat hunched on one of the metal folding chairs set up against the wall, tear-filled tissues in both hands. Except for her, his surroundings resembled a stylish cocktail party, everyone wearing dark, fashionable clothes. Just place drinks in the hands of the little cluster groups standing around chatting, reading the cards on the flowers to see who sent the biggest and most original condolences, whispering to each other about so-and-so over there. Have you heard the latest about ...?

His thoughts parodied T. S. Eliot.

"In the room, the people come and go ..."

He thought to try one last time. "Look, Dad, it's just ... for me"—he cleared his hoarse voice—"that's not Mom."

"That's silly!" His father looked around to see if he had spoken too loudly.

He knew his father understood what he meant. The old wall between them still stood.

"Jesus!" Paul glared at his puzzled-looking father and sister, then put his hands to his face. Why was it so important to them that he look? Why did they even think that stiff, probably powdered and rouged form lying in that shiny, oblong metallic-gray tube was some work of art? His mother was dead. Gone. Couldn't they understand that was not his mother lying there? What good would it do to look at a lifeless shell, washed and made up, injected with chemicals, made to look as though she were sleeping peacefully? That wasn't the image he had or wanted to keep of her.

He had wanted cremation. For him, the whole notion of people gathering together to look at a dead body seemed a holdover from some primitive state from which man had not yet evolved.

His sister said something to him about "Please, do it for Dad," but Paul's anger pushed him into wondering if his mother might be alive now if it weren't for his father.

It was what his dad had said to him over the phone. His mother, complaining of chest pains, had awakened his father, but over the years, he had become accustomed to her having bad nights with various pains. She'd been ill on and off a lot the last few years with one thing and another, but nothing too serious lately, so his father had gone back to sleep. Later, she had awakened him again, this time saying she thought she'd better go to ER; she was having trouble breathing. Probably just her asthma, he had told her, but he agreed to take her. By the time his father dressed and got her to the hospital, the pains had increased. She died ten minutes after they reached the hospital. Massive coronary.

"If only I'd taken her sooner," his father later was to say over and over but always adding, "The doctor said it wouldn't have made any difference." Paul could see his father was shaken and grieving. But with a touch of guilt?

Still, Paul couldn't help wondering if the doctor's words weren't meant to ease his father's pain. Why hadn't his father taken more note of her complaints? As far as Paul could tell, his father had never taken her health issues the way Paul thought he should have.

But then what was his own excuse? Had he proven to be any better? He hadn't seen her in over two years now. Written little. Called a couple of times. Just accepted her usual not feeling well.

Luke should be here. How his mother had loved her only grandson. But he had no idea where Luke was. Hadn't seen or heard from him in three years. Reached eighteen and disappeared. Could be dead, for all the family knew. God, he'd really screwed up raising that kid. So different from Laura.

Some people he didn't know came toward them to express their condolences. Grateful for their approach, Paul quickly excused himself before his father could protest. Laura had moved, so he sat alone on one of the metal chairs in the corner. He closed his eyes, shutting the present out—now with his mother again, that last time—the very last time they'd been alone together …

\* \* \*

"My, this is lovely. I see now why you like it out here," his mother said, her face tilted into the wind, wisps of gray-brown ringlets trying to escape from the blue scarf tied under her chin.

Wearing the old sailing jacket Paul kept on board, she looked small, childlike. She sat slightly hunched, hands deep inside the jacket pockets. About two miles off Santa Barbara, they were doing about eight smooth knots in his Cal-20. The jib and main were set, his mother looked comfortable, and for the first time since leaving the harbor, he was able to relax and enjoy the sail. A bit chilly but a perfect combination of wind and water.

Only recently had he been able to afford to buy the boat, but it was worth the price today just to get out of the house. As usual, Linda was showing what to him was an unwarranted irritation with his mother's visit, but this time, it had taken only two days to surface. His wife never failed to slip into her bitchy, oh-your-mother mood, positioning him in a loyalty tension split he never learned to handle. While his mother never said anything to him, it wasn't difficult to read her face. He felt like the guy tied to two horses, being pulled in different directions.

On this day, Luke and Laura, his mother's real reason for coming so far to visit, were still in school and not in the house to take away some of the uneasiness. He'd finished teaching his morning classes and had come home to grade some student tests he wanted to give back tomorrow. But once in the door, he felt Linda's frigid manner toward his mother building, so to avoid any impending clash, he'd invited his mother to go sailing.

"What's that white building up there, just at the foot of the lower hill?"

He told her.

"Really? It looks different from here." She tried to take in everything. "This is such a lovely way to see the coast!" He smiled at her enthusiasm.

The mountains behind the city stood a clean green from the recent, infrequent rain. The red Spanish-tiled roofs dotted the foothills and then thickened as they spilled down into the city itself, a Mediterranean postcard. He felt himself contacting some of that old rapport he and his mother had once shared that had dissipated over the years with infrequent contact. Yet he felt it. Each slight splash the small boat carved through a wave made his memory more liquid. The dark water holding up the boat hid so much. Remembrances surfaced in random pieces like flotsam and jetsam.

Years before his sister, he and his mother had sat many times by the apartment's front room window, looking into the dark, waiting for the headlights that signaled his dad was home from work.

His dad. For the first ten years or so, more a stranger than a father. Often asleep by the time his dad came home, he saw him only briefly in the mornings and on Sundays. Nice of you to drop by, Dad. He shared in his mother's lonely night vigilance, almost a routine, but in truth, he didn't know his father well enough to miss him or, at that time of his life, to know what he needed to miss. But his mother loved and worried about this man, his father, so he felt loneliness along with her, but mostly for her.

They were lucky his father had a job, his mother often told him. These are hard times, she would tell him. "Your dad has to work late. He'd like to be with us, but he has to work so hard." Paul never really understood why, if his father wanted to be with them, he wasn't. Something about having to catch people home from work in order to collect their insurance premiums. This meant Saturdays and sometimes Sundays, too. If he was to collect, he had to cover his territory. What was it he called it? A debit? So he really learned to love his father through his mother. She was always his father's champion. Always.

"Bye, baby bunting, Daddy's gone a-hunting..."

He tried to remember his father ever playing with him when he was young, doing father-son things. He couldn't. Not a memory.

Well, not true. Once when he was about ten, during some company picnic, a softball game was organized. Paul had embarrassed his dad because he couldn't play ball very well. Other kids had popped fielders, smacked grounders, caught fly balls, knew where to throw the ball. Not Paul. He couldn't stop or catch the ball in the outfield. He struck out every time at bat. "Easy out! Here comes an easy out!" Those words had burned into him with painful laughter, stinging even now.

He had cried angrily in front of everyone. His father's face had shown embarrassment, disappointment, annoyance. Sissy for crying, he saw in his father's eyes. But he had cried because he felt hatred toward his father, hatred for never having played ball with him, hatred for never having shown him how to hit or catch, hatred for making him a weakling, a mama's boy in those strange people's eyes. He wanted his tears to shame his father, too.

They moved around Albany a lot back then. It seemed as soon as he got settled in one place, they would move again, never providing a chance to form many friendships. His early life held periods when his mother seemed his only friend. It was his mother who taught him how to change the plug on an electrical cord, how to hammer a nail, how to mix paint and clean brushes.

In those early years, he knew the people on television better than his father. Matt Dillon from *Gunsmoke*. Little Joe from *Bonanza*. Steve McGarrett, *Hawaii Five-O*. Dick Van Dyke. Lucy. And all those *Million-Dollar Movies* he and his mother shared had introduced him to Fred and Ginger and Tracy and Hepburn. Our second lives.

But the best listening times involved *Your Hit Parade,* when the two of them would sing along to the ten top tunes of the week. He loved to hear his mother sing, convinced she sang well enough to be on the show.

A story told by relatives had developed about how his mother— this was even before she met his father—had beaten a then- unknown Ginger Rogers in a song-and-dance contest. Details were vague. When he used to ask her about it, her hands seemed to fidget. She'd smile, get a nostalgic look, acknowledge it, but just dismiss it as something that happened too long ago to be important.

"So long to *Your Hit Parade* and the wonderful tunes that we played ..."

Arms wrapped around her pulled-up legs, his mother was resting her chin on her knees looking out over the sea for any sign of the whales he had told her she might see. Even now, she still had a slim figure, a dancer's figure. Why hadn't she pursued it? Had being pregnant with him been a part of losing her dream? Had his father kept her from it?

Whatever the reasons, she had sweetly connived to make a dancer of him. He smiled as he remembered her craftiness. What was he—five, six maybe? She had promised him that when he finished that large, ugly brown bottle of cod liver oil with the fish image carved on both sides, he could have anything he wanted. Anything? Yes, anything.

How she'd managed to get him to believe he wanted tap-dancing lessons he'd never know. But he finished the bottle—he still remembered that gag-awful taste—and that's what he got, tap-dancing lessons. If she couldn't be Ginger, maybe she could make him her young Fred, shuffling off to Buffalo. Click, clickety click.

He didn't remember whether or not he was any good. He did remember that the night of his big dance recital, dressed in a little tuxedo his mother had sewn, his dad didn't show up.

Another late working night. Or maybe he didn't want to see a sissy-boy dancer. Soon after that, the lessons stopped. Lack of money or was he a disaster on his feet?

Nancy was born when he was nine, and things changed some. His dad had become some kind of a manager and was home more, but by then, Paul had grown used to the distance between them. Oh, they did some family things together—church activities mostly— and he and his dad got on all right, but something never got a chance to grow. As Paul grew older, it seemed to him that his dad, realizing he had failed with a son, tried to compensate somehow with his daughter. Maybe it was just sibling rivalry, but whenever he and Nancy discussed their father, they seemed to be discussing two different people.

Looking up from the passing gray deep, he regarded his mother. Paul was struck by how she had aged. He'd never noticed before. It took him by surprise, as though he had thought she'd always look the same. Still showing remnants of a face he always thought pretty, her skin looked too pale with brown blotches, her nose seemed a bit wide and red, her green eyes sank into dark circles, and her chin set incorrectly from new teeth. She did not look well.

Somewhere in his desk, he kept an old, faded brown photograph of the two of them when he was about four. A street vendor had taken it on one of their frequent window-shopping walks downtown. She'd sent in the envelope the photographer gave her, and when the picture came, she gave it to Paul. He was holding her hand and stood less than half her size. He wore a little cap with a small peak, a sweater, and shorts. She wore a small flowered hat, set on the side, and a simple, form-fitting dress that came down slightly below her knees. Short, curly hair framed a pretty face. Her eyes looked straight into the camera. He'd kept it all these years. Always, he'd thought of her as she looked in that picture.

The photograph held loving memories. Their occasional lunch at Woolworth's counter.

Sitting on a stool, eating a ham sandwich and drinking a cherry Coke. Window shopping at department stores. Making fudge together, licking the pan, waiting for it to cool and be cut. Making cherry pie for his birthdays because he preferred it to cake.

A sudden slight wave hit the broadside and splashed into the boat, getting his mother's seat wet. She tried to stand but couldn't get her balance and plopped back down.

"Oh dear." She laughed a bit falsely, looking around, not knowing what to do.

"You OK? Are you very wet?" The same concern swept over him that had back when they were on one of their walks, and she fell, skinning her knees, pregnant with Nan. He'd never before seen blood on his mother. For some reason, he'd assumed her discomfort was his fault; he had not protected her enough. For days, he felt and accepted the guilt, even though she had assured him it couldn't possibly have been his fault. He remembered the tear and run in her stocking.

"I'm fine. I'm OK. Really. Just a little wet in the seat, that's all." She pulled at the soaked seat of her slacks. He noticed her frail, skeleton-like hands, fingers gnarled from arthritis, fingers that had sewn most of his early clothes.

"Shall we head back in?" He couldn't let go of the tiller to go below for anything to dry off her seat.

"No. I'm enjoying this. I really am." She tried to brush the dampness from the wet cushion she sat on. Then she gave up and put her face to the wind and sun, closing her eyes. He felt sure he saw true enjoyment, despite the wetness.

A good sport, always. She never complained about much of anything that he could remember. How many times in his life had he heard "You've got the sweetest mother."

Only once could he remember her getting angry with him. It had surprised him. Ann Walker. Yes, he was dating Annie Walker. His junior year. He'd come home later than promised. They'd lost track of time just listening to music on the car radio. His dad was sleeping, he guessed, but his mother was up, waiting, worried. She lashed at him angrily, surprising him.

What were the words? Something like, "You're out necking (does anybody say that anymore?) with that girl while we're home, worried to death about you!" She'd ranted a bit; he remembered mostly her unusual tone.

Startled by her feelings, his defense mechanisms had blurted out the truth, that he and Ann were just good friends, that he'd never kissed her, never even tried to.

Only he didn't tell her how much he wanted to and more. But he was shy, partly afraid of rejection, partly the times; that's just how it was. How different his life might be if he'd been more aggressive, been more aggressive with Ann, with other girls he'd known. How he wished he had been doing what his mother thought!

His mother never said any more about it. He still couldn't figure out why she had reacted as she did that night. Hadn't she liked Ann? Was she worried he might get some girl pregnant? Or was she dumping on him after fighting with Dad? But he had never heard them fight. Not even an unkind word to each other.

The jib fluttered, and the main snapped sharply. He'd fallen off course. His mother looked at him questioningly.

"Just lost the wind for a minute." He adjusted the tiller, and the sails filled again. "Want to head back, Mom? Cold?"

"In a bit. I'm fine, really." He smiled inwardly at the way she always injected a "really," as if she didn't expect to be believed.

She asked him to point out a few more city landmarks, probably in no hurry to get back to the house, at least not until the kids were home from school. He almost started to apologize to his mother for his wife's attitude, but to do that, he'd have to apologize for marrying.

Apologize to your mother for getting married. Now there was a thought. Actually, maybe she should apologize to him. She had raised him. And like the good boy she raised him to be, he had saved himself for the one he would marry. Not too unusual in his day. But look what it got him. It took him years even to think it, but he knew now he'd been living a mistake. What you think you know when you're twenty-one! But surely, he himself must have known even back then. Why else had he been afraid—or was it shame—to tell his parents? Why hadn't he been honest with himself?

He married Linda six weeks after their first time. He knew now it was the sex. Funny. All those frustrating years of waiting, saving himself, hearing about it from others, painfully wanting to so many times, he ended up marrying someone who hadn't waited herself. But she took him some place he'd wanted to go, had never been, and could never come back from. His sexual dam burst with so much release that once opened, he got carried away with the flood. Sex held him captive, albeit a willing one, and brought with it an obligation to marry.

When he had called two months later to tell his parents he was bringing home a wife along with his discharge from the army, his dad let loose with shock, hurt, disapproval, arguments. You're too young. You don't know what you're doing. You'll ruin your life. You've got to finish college. Why didn't you tell us? His dad had surprised him by being more against it than his mother. She had seemed more accepting of it, but then, maybe he only saw in his mother what he wanted to see. It took him a long time to admit his dad had been proven right.

But when he brought her home, they had all played the "nice" game. They accepted his choice on the surface. Linda accepted them on the surface. Of course, he hadn't seen it that way at the time. He'd just assumed they would all live happily ever after. He went back to college, and his wife found a job.

Then something happened after Laura and Luke were born. Money got tight when his wife had to quit work. He had to take fewer classes and work part-time jobs. Patch by patch, his mother and wife began piecing together a quilt of stress. His wife didn't like his mother's taste in clothes she bought or made for the kids. His mother thought the children should say "please" and "thank you" more. His wife resented how "sweetly" his mother talked to the kids. His mother thought his wife talked too harshly when the children did something wrong. His wife accused Grandma of spoiling the kids; their teeth would rot from too many sweets. His mother thought the kids needed more affection and attention. His wife resented the affection the grandmother showed them. She was jealous of his mother.

"They like their grandma better than they like their own mother!" His wife never held in her feelings. His mother bristled in silence. On top of that, his father seemed to take Linda's side and blame his mother for the stress. Gradually, each conflict contributed another patterned square to a suffocating family blanket.

Relief came for a time when he got his degrees, and one of his offers was a teaching position on the West Coast. He wondered now if he hadn't secretly taken the job to get away from the conflicts. With such a low starting salary, he'd had to teach extra night classes and the summer sessions, even taking on some private tutoring. In order to get placed higher on the pay scale, he had to enroll in more state accreditation courses offered in the late evening or on nights he wasn't teaching. During those years, teaching consumed him. But he had loved it all, loved his students, and both found and lost himself in the challenge of it.

During those first years, he could never afford to take his family back to see his parents, so they began inviting the kids back to their home during the summer holidays. His parents used to make trips out a couple of times a year when the children were younger, usually around Easter and Christmas. But that old conflict quilt always got dragged out and thrown over the family.

Feelings got hurt. Tensions mounted.

His dad started to come out less frequently. "Business and all," he'd claim. Now his mother came but once a year, usually alone. Even he himself had grown to dread her visits, the pull in two directions.

"Look! Is that a whale?" His mother pointed with one hand and shaded her eyes with the other.

It was. In fact, two. The grays surfaced very near the boat, their spouts creating fountains.

Then together, their heavy bodies arched effortlessly into a dive, flukes caked with barnacles waving goodbye. From the size of them, they appeared to be a mother and her young calf. The sight was not new to him, but sharing it with his excited mother made it a magical moment.

As they watched the whales at play, slipping easily out of sight, then appearing from nowhere, a wave of truth dampened him.

He had become like his own father.

In avoiding the reality of his mistaken marriage, he had spent too little time with his own children—his son, mostly—by working long hours. He had become what he resented in his own father. Absent. Like his dad, he could blame absence on hard work.

At that moment, he couldn't find any memories of ever playing with his son any more than he could recall memories of his own father playing with him. Even later, when his daughter came, it seemed there was always some excuse.

"Can you play with us, Daddy?"

"No, kids, Daddy's got to grade papers."

"Let's play some ball, Dad."

"Sorry, kid, have to beat the deadline on this journal article."

"Can you take us to the park?"

"Can't. Need to prepare for class tomorrow."

Somewhere along the line, necessary work had become a convenience, a good excuse to avoid his wife and children who, ironically, respected him because he worked so hard for them. But they didn't have to wait up for him to come home like he had with his father; oh no, he just shut himself off in his office, closing the door to them. Like himself, his own children knew their mother more than their father. "Don't bother your dad; he's busy." But what did they really know of him or he of them? What did he know of himself beyond his teaching?

Too old too soon, too wise too late.

His mother had always excused his father's absence, saying he had to work late; times were bad. But maybe that wasn't all. Maybe his dad had been unhappy all those years, using work as an excuse. He'd never thought of his father as the unhappy one, only his mother. But now he saw himself and his father as actually having shared the same pattern of avoidance. Is this why his dad had been so upset when he'd come home married? Did he see history repeating itself?

Paul was off course again, and his mother looked cold huddled in his jacket. He wanted to ask her if his father loved her, if he was a happy man.

"Let's come about and head back in," he suggested.

Back inside the harbor, he brought the boat easily alongside the slip, jumped on the dock, and tied her off. He gave his mother a hand up to the dock, and as she stepped up, she slipped slightly into him, his hand accidentally cupping her left breast, embarrassing him, resurrecting a strange memory—was he six? seven?—half-asleep in his parent's bed, waiting for his father to come home. His mother had leaned over to tell him to go to sleep. Her sleeveless nightgown had fallen loose. He remembered that innocent yet odd, dizzy, erotic feeling as he stared at his mother's naked breasts ...

\* \* \*

"Blessed be the ties that bind ..."

That music. From church so long ago, one of his mother's favorite hymns.

"Please. Come on, now. We have to go down front." Nancy was helping him up from the chair, whispering her words. "It's the last time you'll get to see her."

"Mom?"

It took a moment before he realized where he was and what he was doing. His father, sister, wife, and daughter were walking him toward the gray metal container. One of them was saying something about needing to close the lid so the procession could start. There, again, came that overpowering sickly sweetness of so many blended flowers.

If you spend time hoping someone will suffer the
consequences for what they did to your heart,
then you're allowing them to hurt you a
second time in your mind.

—Shannon L. Adler

# GETTING EVEN

"**H**oney, come look at this email!"
"What is it?"
"Just come look."

Even though Evan had retired from teaching English two years ago, he still received email notices from the college personnel office. This particular email took him where he'd prefer not to go again. Still, his wife would want to see this.

Liz leaned over him from behind, hands on his shoulders, and read from his computer screen:

> **It is with deep sadness that we learned of Dr. Richard Longfield, one of the college's longest-tenured faculty members, passing away this morning, Tuesday, August 6, after a long illness. Professor of sociology, Dr. Longfield taught here for thirty-one years. His wife, Mary Lee, and his son, David, survive Dr. Longfield. We will share details about any memorial services as they become available. On behalf of the college, we extend our sympathies and condolences to Dr. Longfield's family on his passing.**

"Well, then," Liz said after a moment. "The rumors about cancer were true." She must have felt Evan's body tense and began rubbing his shoulders. He reached back and put his hands on hers, wondering about her reaction to the news. His eyes stared at the words on the screen, but they were no longer his focus, only the memory beyond the words.

Evan knew it would be a lie to say he felt much sympathy, if any. Dick Longfield never became a friend during their twenty or so shared years on campus. In fact, he thought Longfield a bit overbearing, a man who loved to exhibit his erudite vocabulary, whether spouting off his views at faculty meetings or speaking individually with students. The Dr. in front of Dick's name had gone to his head, and he believed it granted him special status. Seldom without an empty briarwood pipe in hand, Longfield had wielded it like a baton to accompany his speech. Very affected. Rather odd on a smoke-free campus. So Evan had avoided contact with him whenever possible. Until Longfield had made it impossible.

That unwanted personal history between them still disturbed him, and to this day, he did not understand its source. Why Longfield had targeted him and his wife remained an unfathomable mystery.

He read the email again. Now Longfield was dead. What were his feelings?

Should he have a moment of there-but-for-god-go-I feelings? He didn't. In all honesty, he leaned more toward celebration than mourning at the news. But before he had time to feel any shame, another email popped up on the screen, this one by a department colleague of Longfield's:

> **I was fortunate to share my office with Dick. I learned something new with each conversation. He was a brilliant, wonderful colleague. My sympathies to his family.**

Another followed:

> **Richard was very kind and gentle from the moment I met him as he welcomed me into the campus community. I have always found him to be a joy to interact with, and I honor his life and contribution to us all.**

Yet another and then still others kept popping up like these:

**I, too, echo the many sentiments offered about a great colleague and a man who was the face of excellence at this institution. Dick connected with his students. He reached out to them and reached into their hearts and minds to inquire, to look, to invite, to learn, to understand what made them tick and where he might find ways to intersect, interject, interact.**

Liz quit rubbing his shoulders as they read the dead man's tributes. While Liz said nothing, Evan knew she must be sharing some of his feelings and memories.

"My god, can you believe this bullshit?"

The uncontrolled anger raging through his body undid his wife's massaging efforts. All these sickening eulogies about Richard reawakened the wrath he thought he had repressed. He realized that when someone died, the negative attributes were often subdued by the positives. But what a load of crap this was! That was the only way to state it. Dick Longfield was a real dick, and nobody was coming close to stating the truth, not as he and Liz knew it.

Liz took his head in her hands and gently turned his face to hers, looked at him, and sighed.

"The man's dead, honey. None of it matters anymore."

"Really? After what he's done to us, you'd let people keep thinking he was this wonderful ... asshole?"

"Does it really matter anymore?"

"It does to me. I can't let him get off so easily, not even in death."

"Just drop it. Let people think what they want. Think of his family and how they feel right now. They don't know anything about what he did. What's done is done."

"No. What's done is what people have to know."

Anxious, he turned back to his computer and started his own email tag, wanting to add some reality regarding this man's character.

**So, our revered Professor Longfield is dead. If what everyone is saying in praise of Richard, the "dick" I knew, is true, then he fits a classic case of schizophrenia. Here is what I know about this man. With no cause or reason that I ever understood, he approached me in the hall outside**

**my office one day and accused me of having an affair with his wife. God's truth, I had no idea what he was talking about, but he wouldn't accept my denial. I knew nothing of his personal life, let alone his wife. I'd met her twice, both times at campus functions, and never saw her again. I didn't even remember her name. So why did he select me for his fantasy? I never found out. But it didn't end there.**

He stopped composing as the unsettling memories sprang back. At first, Evan had tried to dismiss Longfield's accusation; he was obviously looking for someone to blame for his wife's affair. If she was even having an affair. Who knew if it was true? Evan didn't. So he shrugged it off, thinking maybe Dick was going through male menopause. Evan had no interest in becoming involved in Longfield's life. But that wasn't to be.

A week or so later, when I came home, Liz confronted me with an anonymous letter she had received, asking her if she knew her husband was having an affair with a colleague's wife.

"You don't believe this, do you?"

"Should I?"

"Of course not!" The accusation and threat to his innocence sent him into a red zone, and his voice rose as he spouted his defense.

"Calm down. I believe you. But what's this about? Who do you think would send such a thing?"

Evan started to say he had no idea, but then he did.

"Dick Longfield. That son of a bitch still thinks I'm having a thing with his wife."

"Has he said any more to you since the first time he confronted you?"

"No. But it has to be Dick. Who else?"

While Liz took the first letter in stride, Evan couldn't explain to her or himself why Longfield accused him as the guilty one.

Then, every day for over two weeks, another letter of accusation would arrive, each one addressed to Liz, each one suggesting she should be worried about what her unfaithful husband was doing to her marriage as well as to his colleague's. The anonymous author suggested Liz should do something about it. The letters were typed, sent in non-distinguishing envelopes. It grew to be something they could no longer laugh off.

With each letter, Evan could see his wife's uncertainty building. She wanted to believe him but couldn't help feeling disturbed by the accusations and began wondering if she should be suspicious, although she tried hard not to be. Still, she caught herself becoming sullen and a bit sharp in tone around him.

"I am not having an affair," he kept repeating. "Please believe me."

"Do you still think it's this Richard person?"

"Who else could it be? He straight out accused me to my face."

"Explain to me why he is doing this."

"I honestly don't know. I only know it isn't true."

"What did you ever do to him? Is he getting even for something?"

"No. We're not even in the same department. I barely know him."

"Confront him. Tell him to stop, or you'll report him."

"He knows I have no proof. I can't prove the letters are from him. And he'd deny it anyway."

"Well, do something. I can't take this anymore."

"How can I defend myself against a lie?"

He heard tears shed behind closed doors.

Evan understood why she might be questioning his innocence, but he felt angry that she was developing suspicions. A tension grew between them. He understood why she couldn't help but wonder if there was any merit in the letters. And maybe, he thought, his trying so hard to prove the letters wrong made him look guilty. To help ease the situation, he made it a point to be where he said he was when he wasn't home. He went out of his way to give his wife no cause for suspicion. Still, their home took on a somber air, and he couldn't take it anymore, either.

Evan determined to end Richard's lunacy and confronted him in his office for a showdown. With the office door open, Evan watched Richard as he sat back in his desk chair, all smiles, pointing his pipe at a female student he was talking to, lost in his scholarly demeanor.

Why did this man want to destroy my life?

When Longfield noticed Evan standing there and saw the look on his face, Longfield immediately dismissed the student. After she left, he tapped his tobaccoless pipe on his hand.

"Yes?" He swiveled in his chair to face Evan.

Evan just stared at him for a moment, thinking of a thousand curse words to throw at him, but he just got to the point. "I know you're sending those letters to my wife, and I'm telling you to stop, or you're going to see that pipe somewhere besides in your mouth."

"Letters? What letters?" His pretentious voice didn't hide his guilt, and his smirk was the real giveaway. He placed his pipe in the corner of his mouth. I had to refrain myself from what my mind envisioned doing with his damn pipe.

"Don't play with me. I'm not having any affair with your wife. I don't know why you think I am, but I'm not. Your letters are upsetting my wife, and I want you to stop. If your wife is having an affair, why do you think it's me, anyway?"

"Really, I don't know what you're talking about." He turned from Evan and started shuffling some papers on his desk.

"You know damn well what I'm talking about, you son of a bitch."

Evan stood there, frustrated, ineffectual, looking at the back of his tormentor's head, wanting to strangle him.

"Just back off, understood?" Shaking, Evan left before he really lost it.

\* \* \*

Back to composing his email, Evan added:

**Thankfully, the letters did stop. But then came the phone calls with no one on the line. The phone would ring; we'd answer, and no one responded. Sometimes, there would be breathing, sometimes just silence and a hang-up. I had no proof, but it could only have been Dick's doing; he even indicated a kind of confession when I confronted him again, this time on the calls. He held his hand up to his ear pantomiming a phone call, mouthing something I didn't get. I could see how he enjoyed his little charade. Finally, the calls stopped. Either he got worried he'd gone too far, or he discovered who was having an affair with his wife and started pestering that person.**

He stopped composing again and revisited his last encounter with Longfield. Not long after the letters and phone calls stopped, Longfield stuck his head in Evan's office, grinning as if he held some secret.

"How's your sex life going?"

"What the hell, Richard?"

What was it going to be this time? That vile grin of his again.

"Word is you can't get it up."

Evan looked at him, completely baffled.

"What the hell are you talking about?"

"A mutual student of ours tells me you couldn't get it up with her."

He leaned against the doorframe, arms crossed, eyes bright with the accusation. All Evan could think to say came out. "You're really sick, you know that?"

"She's laughing about it. Told me how embarrassed you were." Longfield gestured his damn pipe in the air.

"Jesus, Richard. What's with you, anyway? What is your damn obsession with my sex life?" He shook his head and watched Longfield relish his moment. "OK, I know you want me to ask. Who supposedly told you this?"

"Oh, no supposedly. Emphatically for real. You know very well who she is." He strutted away as if he'd won a Pulitzer Prize story, softly singing, "He can't get it up; he can't get it up in the morning," to the tune of the reveille bugle call.

Evan did not know "very well" who it was because he had made it a rule his whole teaching career to never get overinvolved with his female students. He wondered if some student really made this claim against him, or was Richard's demented mind at work again? And why, why was this man zeroing in on Evan? Was he off his meds or something? He was certainly off in some dizzy whimsy land, but he was taking Evan and his wife with him.

He'd had enough and caught up with the bastard in the hall, grabbed his shoulder, jerked him around, and yanked his pipe from his mouth. It must have hurt his teeth because his hand went to his jaw and made some sound that Evan hoped was connected to pain.

Before Richard caught up with the shock, Evan pointed the pipe at him like a pistol and said, not caring who might be in the hall, "Here's what going to happen, you son of a bitch. You are going to get off my back with your sick fantasies. If you accuse me of one more thing, if you even talk to me again, on or off campus, I am going to send anonymous letters to your wife accusing you of diddling your students. Since this female student and you are so intimate you can freely discuss my supposed sex life, I'll bet it's you who's having the affair with her. Of course, that's it! I will write letters to your dean, to the college president, to the editor of the local paper suggesting a certain sociology professor is taking sexual advantage of his female students for grades. And believe me, there will be no doubt it is you. And I'll do it in such a way they'll never suspect it's me. You've taught me well."

At last, Evan saw Longfield lose his composure. His expression changed, and the arrogance melted from his face as he tested the movements of his pained chin. Evan's first thought was "My god, I've awakened him from some dream. Now he'll probably sue me for physical damages."

Wordless, he stared at Longfield, feeling a growing sense of power being transferred from one man to the other until he knew this was a moment he would never get to experience again.

He started to give back Longfield's pipe. Instead, he dropped it on the floor at his feet. To retrieve it, Longfield had to bend down. When he started to rise, Evan pushed down hard on his shoulders, forcing Longfield to kneel, keeping him there a moment.

"Grovel, asshole," he said, enjoying a newfound self, then him let loose.

Feeling redeemed, Evan turned and went back to his office. He sat there feeling his shaking body slowly release the built-up tension.

From that moment on, the accusations stopped, and they never heard from Longfield again.

He summarized all this in his email and then added:

**So you people are sending praises and sympathies to his family? What about sympathy for my wife, for her waves of tears and the mistrust that nearly drowned my marriage, the torment and suspicions my wife had to endure? How many of you colleagues praising this "gentleman on**

campus" know this sordid side of the man? Anyone else willing to come forth with comments on the real Richard Longfield?

He paused and reread what he'd written: all true, the perfect opportunity to expose Dr.

Psycho. How could all those tributes to a crazy man be so far off the mark? By sending this email, he felt pleased, his outrage vindicated. He was righting a wrong. And yes, proving to him that revenge was sweet.

Evan took in a deep breath, held it, his stiffened middle finger poised over the Send button.

Some people feel the rain; others just get wet.

—Roger Miller

# WINTER BREAK

" **P**rofessor Stephens, I've got a question. Like, I mean, what makes Joyce's 'Araby' such a great story, anyway? I don't get it."

Oh, great start. Who said that? … Oh yes, the one on my left with the baseball cap on backward. Why do they do that? Silly.

"Me, either."

Uh-oh, another one … somewhere back there. Couldn't tell who. Not a good class beginning …

"Yeah, like, you know, it's really boring."

"It doesn't make sense."

"Nothing happens."

Here they come. The inevitable rumbles rippling 'round the room. Lord help me, why did I assign this story? After thirty years, I should know better than to start with Joyce. Why, why do I keep hoping? … Look at them … forty fidgeting freshman waiting for me to tell them what they've read, what's important to know. Never again. There must be some seekers out there…. OK, take a deep breath … teach …

"Well, let's see if we can't discover why it's considered a great story." Start simply, now. "Let's begin with the plot. Could someone summarize the plot of 'Araby' for us?" Scan the classroom for a willing face. Wish I knew their names better. Naturally, no one's volunteering. Maybe I should go back to a seating chart. What's that kid's name over in the corner scrunched down in his seat?

Never looks up. Don't even know what his face looks like … always scribbling in his notebook. If he'd look up, I'd call on him. "Hey, you, the scribbler."

Ha, shake him up a bit. And that one, sitting back there messing with his iPhone wired to his ear, chewing gum in time with whatever he's listening to. Wouldn't hear me if I called on him. So call on the backward baseball cap. Yes, he started this … throw the ball back at him.

Go ahead, he's looking at you. Nod. "How about you? Can you summarize the plot for us?"

"Me?"

Ha, look at him rise from his slouch gotcha. "Yes." Give a little smile. "You. Just state the plot as simply as you can." If you even know what a plot is, which I doubt. That's it; sit up in your seat, struggle. Didn't you read the assignment?

"Well, like, all I got outta this story is it's about this weird kid who, like, wanted to go to some fair or bazaar or somethin' like that. And this girl—his friend's sister, I think—sort of like takes advantage of his, you know, crush on her."

No, no, not the story—the plot, the plot. Lord help me; he doesn't even have the story right.

"Excuse me, sir, but what he said really confuses me now."

Now who's that? Ah, yes, the thick-lipsticked young lady who wears silver rings on every finger. Think her name's Sharon. Look at her, flopping a half-raised arm held up by the other arm. All that silver must be heavy.

"Yes?" Jeezus H, now where's this going to lead?

"Confused about what exactly?" How can she use her hands with so many rings wedged on her fingers? Is that one on her thumb, too?

"Well, I'm not sure. I mean, like, is what he just said a plot? I mean, 'cause I thought a plot was, like, sort of an outline, you know, just the series of events that make up the action of the story."

Well, now, can this be … ?

"That's what I learned in high school English, anyway."

It was also defined in the reading assignment. "Yes, you're quite right. What we heard was not a plot; in fact, not even the story, really. At least not the one I've read several times." Careful, you're getting rude. Smile a little. "Would someone else like to try stating the plot of "Araby? Look expectantly at the ring girl. Ah, she's thumbing through her text … pretending, maybe. "Oh, she wore rings on her fingers, bells on her toes." There, the older man in the second row off to the left a bit. Was his hand up slightly? He's looking. Nod at him to speak. Christ, those jaundiced-looking fingertips…smoker, no doubt. And that tattoo. How long up his arm? Hasn't said a word in class yet this term.

"Well, I may be wrong, but it seems to me this is basically a little puppy love story. You know, boy sees girl, boy falls in love with girl, boy tries to impress girl, but instead of getting girl or losing girl, he learns something about himself."

Falling in love with love is falling for make believe. I remember the trouble with teaching this story last year … and the year before. Why? Why? What made me think I could do it this term? Wonder why he's taking this class. Name's Petersen, I think, with an e. Ah, the jeweler's daughter's raising her hand …

"Yeah, OK, now that's the plot, right? What he just said?"

Why, look, she's wearing silver earrings, too. "Ahh, why, yes. I suppose you could say that's a fair analysis of the plot." Be careful here; you weren't really listening. Cover yourself. "On one level."

"Yeah, well, OK."

And now, sports fans, back to the backward baseball cap.

"But what does the kid learn about himself? I mean, I can't see where he learned anything."

Maybe if you turned your hat around …

"Sir, isn't the story really about disillusionment?"

Ooo, a new voice. All our heads turn toward the young woman on the far right near the window. Ah, yes, the intelligent-looking one. Justin, Kathy Justin. Excellent first essay … best in that first batch. Good thesis, strong support, well organized. Think she's the one, anyway.

Pretty, too. Lovely doe-shaped eyes beneath those glasses … soft brown hair…

What would she look like without those large rims? Take 'em off, take 'em off, cried the boys from the rear. Christ, I can't concentrate. "Ah, disillusionment, yes, go on, please." Help me out here.

Don't fail me; I need you.

"Well, the unnamed narrator is obviously looking back, telling the story from his adult perspective and sees himself as, here, let me read..."

My God, she's going to quote from the text. She's actually read the story.

"'A creature driven and derided by vanity.' See, he imagines himself in love with his friend Mangan's sister, imagines himself going on a quest to romantic Araby, bringing back something like a silver chalice to his love, only to be disillusioned by the shoddy Araby bazaar, which brings him back to earth regarding who he is and his naive quest."

Oh God, why can't you give me a class full of students like this one? Lovely mind, lovely face, lovely body ... body? Dismiss the thought ...

"Wow, now how'd you get all that out of this story?"

The backward cap revisited. Look at the way he looks at her. Ah, you like that, don't you, boy? You'll probably hit on her after class I know what you want, and it isn't her brain.

"So what's the big deal, then? I still don't see what makes this story so great. I mean...."

Uh-oh, over there. Right across from the intelligent one—the girl with her sunglasses pushed with fashionable correctness up into her hair. In white tennis shorts every day those smooth, tanned legs. I'd show them off, too. Always crossed, one pumping up and down, distracting me, maybe on purpose. Those curved, polished calves, up along those smooth, solid thighs. A piece of art. Oh, lovely youth, what a waste. Lovely legs. What's wrong with me?

Having bizarre feelings.

"Why doesn't Joyce just tell us all that without making it so hard to understand?"

Oh, lovely, vacuous youth. Stick it to her. "The 'big deal,' my dear"—easy, watch your tone—"has to do with the art—yes, the art—with which Joyce tells us this story of an epiphany, which

many of us, even some of you, must, I hope, someday experience."
You're being mean. Calm down; don't lose it. It's so warm in here.
Are the windows open? Feeling…feeling lost …

"What's an epiphany?"

Oh, another tiny voice in the front row wilderness timidly
ventures forth. Ah, look, a sweet young thing. Innocence personified
in that open, fresh face. Denise something. A quiet one, obviously
listening, struggling to follow, worries about grades, I'll bet. Pen
poised to capture my erudition. Be Socratic. Throw the question
back at the class.

"Good question. Someone? Anyone care to define?" Let's see
what I get this time. Yes, a weak hand halfway up. The older, stout
woman in the second row. Hair in a bun, very motherly looking…
isn't class time about over? I don't want to be here. "Yes, please, go
ahead." A returning student, no doubt. Children grown, doing what
she couldn't finish when she was young because of her motherly
duties. Her husband's probably left her for a younger woman.

"Well, I know in a religious sense, an epiphany is a revelatory
manifestation of a divine being. But in literature, I think it refers
to a sudden understanding or perception of a reality of something
through intuitive means. I don't know if I'm saying it clearly; I'm
not very good at expressing myself."

Mother, you're doing just fine, go on, go on, don't stop. Teach
us. Help me.

"Well, the boy's disillusionment with the bazaar brought about
an epiphany, I think. His awareness that he has fooled himself
about the girl and his romantic idea of Araby."

Yes, yes, hope still springs eternal. A student lives.

"Excuse me, but …"

Oh no. That one. Dressed for a fashion show every day. Does
your father own a clothing store? Can't you shut the fuck up, and let
Mother go on? You're interrupting a voice in the wilderness.

"Are we going to have to know this on a test?"

You may look good on the outside, but honey, I know your brains
are between your legs and that you had an affair with my young
office mate last term … in my office, for Chrissakes. Oh yes, I've got
your number. Play dumb with her. "Have to know what, exactly?"

Did they do it on the floor? On his desk? My desk? Probably on my desk … the ultimate insult. My office mate thinks he's supposed to mate in my office. Not me. Never had an affair with a student. Hear about it all the time. No fringe benefits all these years. Why not me? Thirty years of dealing with their brains, never got dealt a body. What is it about him? His students are always hanging around the office. Mr. Popularity, my office mate. Why not me?

"I mean, like, what she just said. Are we gonna have to define whatever that word is, *efifany?*"

*That* word will definitely not be on a test. "Epiphany." Put it on the chalkboard. *"E-P-I-P-H-A-N-Y."*

"Yeah, whatever."

Whatever? Yes, definitely whatever. Whatever happened to teaching? Whatever happened to the days when students were bright, interesting, studious, well read? My face is getting hot. Were they ever … ? I've been doing this too many years. Were there ever good old days? I don't know any more. What's happening to me? I can't take any more classes like this. Why didn't I get to tangle with Miss Whatever? Why? Why wasn't it me who had you? Look at her … juicy Lucy. It's not your brain I want, either. Admit it … you're jealous. Oh, stop now, collect yourself. Not true. Be a teacher. Teach. But what was the question? Oh yes.

"Don't you think *epiphany* might just be a good word to know? Its significance is certainly tied to Joyce's story, wouldn't you say?" Control, control. You're raising your voice. Mind your tone now. Teach.

Teach. I don't think I can anymore. Nevermore, quoted the big black bird.

"Well, ah, I guess. But …"

Oh, such a sigh. Poor dear. Look at her face. She looks stunned. This must be so hard for you.… . For her? What about me? I want out of here. Let me out of here…

"I still don't understand the boy's e- … e- …"

Look at the board. That's it. There it is, spelled out for you. Shouldn't be too difficult to read.

"Epiphany."

God, if only you paid as much attention to your brain as you do your looks, you'd be brilliant. How much time is left? Don't look at the clock. "Would someone else like to explain for her how you view the epiphany in the story?" Who cares, really? No one. I don't even care anymore. I'm tired of the struggle. Tired, so tired of teaching, fighting the good battle. I need help here. Someone. Nothing's coming together. Falling apart. My epiphany … sick of Joyce, sick of trying. Feeling sick. It's so hot. My armpits are dripping. Wipe your forehead with your handkerchief.

"What about the story's symbolism? I mean …"

Who said that? Who said that? Where are you? My head feels funny. Lightheaded. Better sit down …

"Isn't the title a symbol of something?"

Ah, yes, there he is. That tall, thin kid, slouched in his seat. A wool navy watch cap over his ears, tapping his yellow pencil against his jaw, making a hollow sound. You dumb-ass kid— didn't you just hear my question? Are you deliberately changing the subject? We're trying to talk epiphany here, not symbolism. What the hell do you care about symbolism anyway? What I'd like to do with that pencil. Answer him. "Eh, symbolism, yes, well … we'll … ah, we'll … ah, get to … ah …" Almighty shit, I'm losing it. Hold on. "… Symbolism in a moment, but right now let's stick to … uh, what were we talking about?" I want to kill him. "Oh yes, the epiphany issue. OK? Anyone?" Sweet Jesus, where do these Neanderthals come from? Who passed them on? Yes, that's it; look down, all of you, and hide in your books. Look again at the story you haven't even read, let alone studied. Why did I assign this story? What am I doing here? This is not teaching. Where has it gone? I'm a rubber band stretched too tight. The pressure, the pressure. I need help. Help me. "How about you, Mother? You were saying something about the epiphany in the story, weren't you?"

"Sorry, but did you just call me Mother?"

Oh. My. God. Did I just call her mother? All that tittering around the room … yes, I guess I did. They hate me. They see me slipping, and they love it. Uh-oh, be tactful. Get it back, get it back. "Did I? Sorry, no offense meant. If it was. Offensive, I mean." Oh God, I'm groping. So hot. "You just seem … very motherly; in fact, you remind me of my mother. When she was younger, of course." What are you talking about? Back off, now; don't overkill. Too late. You're already dead. You're finished. Say good night, Gracie.

"Well, no, I'm not offended, but I'm not a mother, either. I'm a nun, actually."

Mother Superior, no doubt. In disguise. Here for my crucifixion. What do you say now, teacher? Oh, the class is really enjoying this one. Look at the way they are looking at me. "Ahh, really?" Oh, great comeback, dipshit. "Well, you … you seem to have a good understanding of the story. Would you like to add anything else to your comments?" I hope you will 'cause, Mama, I'm sinking fast here.

"Well, actually, I have a question. Do you think the conversation early in the story where the boy promises to bring the girl a gift really takes place, or is it only a figment of his mind, a mental extension of his romantic views?"

"Good question. Really good question." What did she just say? Lord, it's hot. Isn't it hot?

That old rugged cross. Used to sing that in church. Pull yourself together now. This isn't church. Hang on. "Anyone want to share your views?" Relax, take deep breaths. It's almost over. Has to be almost over. Can't read the clock. Everything's blurry. Weak knees. Lean on the desk.

"Could that be an example of symbolism?"

Him again. He's tapping his pencil against the other cheek now. Little twit. Are you bald under that watch cap? Do you have ears? Are you hiding something? Are you a gang member? That hat is a symbol. You, you, you are a symbol … of imbecility. Of the death of teaching. So hot. The death of my teaching. Do I mean *depth* or *death*?

"Could … what be?" I forgot the question.

"What she just said. Could that be an example of symbolism?"

What she just said! Oh, clever fellow. "Why don't you tell us how you define symbolism?" There, that'll keep you busy. Defend yourself for a moment. Blather on. Stumble around, get us all confused, make me spend the rest of the class trying to uncomplicate what is meant by symbolism. Every semester is getting worse. Could retire today if I had a dollar for every student who wants to know what's important for the test. It wasn't always thus. It used to be lovely. Now ... now ... it's so hot. My shirt is soaked. The pain in my head... my heart. I've lost it.

"So, is what he said a good definition of symbolism? I mean, that's not what I learned in high school English, anyway."

"What?" Oh God, I didn't even hear how Watch Cap defined symbolism. What's happening to me? Now what is Silverado asking?

"Are we gonna have to know the definition of symbolism on a test?"

Oh God.

"Wait. I still don't understand why the narrator wants to go to the bazaar."

What? Who ... who said that?

"And why doesn't he buy anything when he gets there?"

"Who said that?" Did I say that? What's happening here? You're crowding me. What do you want from me? I can't breathe. Air ... more air. Dizzy. Hot.

"What's the role of the narrator's uncle in the story?"

Take a guess. Can't you guess, you idiots? Don't look at me like that. Why are you looking at me like that? Didn't you read the story? Figure it out. Stay back. So hot. Get away from me. What do you want from me? I've given ... there's no more to give. I'm empty.

"Can we talk about imagery in 'Araby'?"

"You're all trying to mix me up. I know. *Oh, don't think I don't know!*" Yes, yes, oh yes, let's talk; we can talk about imagery, likeness, simile, facsimile, resemblance, semblance; oh yes, let's talk about that; let's talk about your lack, yes. "You ... you semblance of a class ... " Your lack of resemblance to anything close to real students, thinking students, students who want to learn for the sake of learning. *"Where have you gone?"* Students who are interested enough in the world and their place in it to learn to read well, to learn to read a story more than once to understand it, to think, yes, *"Think."* Oh, a foreign word to many of you, I know. *"Pensez."*

But to think about what you read, not wait for me to tell you what a story means, why it is great, what's on a test. Yes, yes, there are always one or two of you who are truly students, "like Mother and…and Glasses over there," but never enough of you. Never enough, not anymore. "Where have you all gone?" And let's talk about why I never had an affair with any of my students. "Tell me." Was I wrong thinking it was dishonorable, not knowing even now why, not really. "I just wanted to be a good teacher." Did I miss my chances? What am I lacking? I'm gutless, or do I have bad breath? Wasn't I good once? I tried, lord I tried. Teaching is so hard I just wanted to give "your minds" the attention I should have given my own children but didn't because I wanted to be a good teacher. "Loving some of you even—and the hours I put in, grading, grading, grading, preparing, preparing, preparing." Seven days a week.

"Sir?"

Mostly essays that deserved no time because you gave them no time. Essays that needed to be rewritten so shallow so dull so lacking in truth oh the time I gave my life I gave it's so hot still none of you hot girls sitting in the front rows ever "spread your legs" to show me you weren't wearing panties oh yes don't think I haven't heard those stories all these years of teaching but it's never happened to me why I don't know I just don't know I've spread myself for you. "Teacher, teacher, I declare, I don't see no underwear." Mindless, mindless. Spread too thin. Not far apart. It's so warm. Where's the air? "Between the legs of life lies the lay of the land, you know." That's alliteration, not stagnation. I still love you, I do; even though I call you names, I don't mean it. You've been my life. My love, really. I don't understand what's happening.

"Are you OK, Dr. Stephens?"

Thank you for asking, Mother. "You…students…." Don't you want to learn? Don't you want to speak up in class take responsibility don't hate school hate me fail me a semblance of a teacher why how laughable semblance talk about semblance I thought I could be a priest a high priest of literature and bring a silver chalice to teaching a life-giving communion yes Joyce I too imagined … "And let me quote Joyce: 'I imagined that I would bear my chalice safely through a throng of foes.'" Are you the foe, or am I wanting an intense romance with teaching with my students with Mangan's sister and all my unknowing loves who were kissed by lamplight wanting to share joys and pains my appreciation my love of literature but to what to whom murdered by scatterbrains by heads where all the lights are out nobody home goodbye gone home dead-end cul-de-sac like the boy Mangan. I can't handle it any more. *"I'm being driven out of the temple!"* My honor gone for what to whom so what I'm a rusty bicycle pump derided by vanity yes vanity thy name is woman the Great God Dissemblance has struck with might what matters is not purity of heart but shoddy stalls of disillusionment. To be or not to be the Sheik of Araby. What a ridiculous question.

"Stay back! Sit down, all of you! You can't have any more of me. It's so hot! It's all too late, isn't it? You don't believe I once loved you. All for naught. It's time for the Bizz-zaar! Let's go, gang, my troops, my wards, my parishioners, my fellow travelers on the road to art and humanity. It's important you care!

"Hey, look! On the wall. Look at the clock, class. Why are its hands spinning, spinning so fast, so fast? Round and round it goes, and where it stops ... Who's playing with the clock?

Dissemblance? Oh yes, it's a symbol. Time, you see, is out of joint. My time is up. I diss you now. Class dis-missed."

"And, yes, oh yes, this will definitely be on the final."

The song is ended but the melody lingers on.

—Irving Berlin

W. Royce Adams is the author of the Rairarubia Series, *The Computer's Nerd, Me & Jay, Jay,* and two collections of short stories, *Against the Current, Scar Song: Stories and a novel, As Time Goes By.* Visit www.wroyceadams.com

www.ingramcontent.com/pod-product-compliance
Lightning Source LLC
Chambersburg PA
CBHW021121130626
46554CB00002B/813